Life is But a Dream

Christine Neligan

© Christine Neligan 2011

ISBN 978-1-871992-25-0

British Library Cataloguing in Publication Data
Christine Neligan 2011
Life is But a Dream

Published by Oasis Press
Hall Mews
Clifford Road
Boston Spa
West Yorkshire
LS23 6DT
UK
www.oasishumanrelations.org.uk

Printed by
Quacks Books
Petergate
York YO1 7HU

Contents

To
Paddy,
Matthew, Cathy and Simon,
and Abi

truly the most wonderful family
a woman could ever belong to

Family Tree

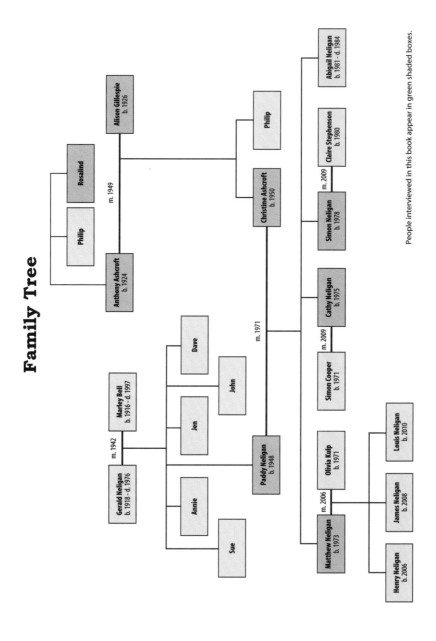

People interviewed in this book appear in green shaded boxes.

Introduction

I have written this book as a tribute to my daughter, Abi, as well as to the rest of my family. Abi died suddenly in 1984. Soon afterwards I realised that everyone in our family had a sense of isolation and, in time, I knew I needed to find a way to capture how each one of us felt in order to understand more. One of the things I discovered is that the process of bereavement is a very personal and unique experience for those involved. I then realised that our journey might be of interest and help to others, and so I made the step towards publishing.

The sudden nature of Abi's death provoked many questions for us all. As parents we wondered about the hospital's responsibility and this was further complicated for us because my husband, Paddy, was a consultant at the same hospital. Some of the feelings raised at that time are strong even now, but we have both reached a point where we accept what happened and realise we have to leave any questions behind and get on with our lives.

Much of the content of this book is informal and conversational in style because it is drawn from transcribed interviews with key members of the family. Each family member's chapter consists of the transcribed conversation followed by my own reflections, wonderings, realisations, thoughts and the wider questions that were raised for me.

At the beginning of each interview I experienced feelings of nervousness (as did those I was interviewing) because my questions were returning us to a very distressing time in our lives and revisiting feelings of grief. I was also unsure of how they would react to the questions I was going to ask. In the event, the experience was helpful, cathartic and allowed us all to understand more about the whole story.

It has taken me some time to bring this together, years in fact, and because of the length of time, the interviews reflect life as it was for that individual then. Now, all our lives are different. Most of us have different jobs, all our three children have married and Paddy and I now have three grandchildren.

One thing I know beyond any doubt, without Abi this book would never have existed.

One

Life is but a Dream...

Abi died on a wet November day in 1984 just a few weeks before her third birthday.

As I begin to write this, we are 22 years on. A life-time has gone by; the life Abi would have had. Who would she have been? What difference would she have made to our family, to our relationships with one another, to us as individuals? Where might we be living? What might we all have done with our lives which would have been different? What would we have achieved? Would we be happier?

I've thought about this, as I know all of my family have over the years. I've wondered so many times - what was the point of her life; what did she bring? I know she brought immense happiness to us, and a huge measure of healing after a traumatic period in our lives following my stillbirth in July 1980. It seemed when Abi was born that we could continue on with our contented lives, putting that trauma behind us.

Every year as we approach 16th November (the anniversary of her death), my thoughts turn back to 1984. I remember the weather we experienced then, the kinds of things I was doing, what our children were up to. Seeing children having fun with 5th November getting nearer brings back memories of the bonfire and fireworks display we went to that year: the cold of the evening, the dampness in the air, the smell of the burning wood, the sight and sound of fireworks – and that little girl on her

1

father's shoulders, wondering what it was all about. A child of almost three can't remember previous Bonfire Nights so it was all a new experience for her.

The picture and memory I have of that happy family – parents, two sons and two daughters – the 'perfect' family; children planned and spaced out as we wanted them. Intelligent, energetic, loving children. And now knowing how soon that was to be shattered.

It took many years, much hard work and reflection for me to realise that Abi has given me an incredible amount through the devastation and grief of her death, as well as the absolute joy of her as my daughter and her contribution to our family.

But my purpose in writing this book is not solely to focus on that day, or even on Abi. The passage of time in the years after Abi died, my understanding and learning about grief and bereavement eventually led me to train as a counsellor so that I could perhaps help others who had been affected by significant events in their lives. I later went on to work as a facilitator of programmes and courses that enabled others to develop the skills themselves so they could, in turn, help others. Whilst this whole process sounds simple, it was immensely challenging at times and spanned many years. It has been incredibly rewarding for me and has helped me in many ways. Increasingly I realise that my children, including those I have lost, and the work I have put into being a mother are the most important achievements in my life.

You might not know me, or my family, but my intent is to share what joy and sorrow mean, how we coped in our own ways, as well as the impact of Abi's life and death on our family. I hope that anyone reading this will understand our story and maybe get some help from it. I hope, too, that it will give some insight into the feelings people experience through the death of a child, as well as understanding how people learn to cope with and move through such an experience.

I want to create something now to honour both Abi and us as a family. I want to be able to have a tangible record to hand down to my grandchildren, and generations to come, to describe how it was. I have the idea that this is our 'family Bible', forming a link with the ancestors. This book will contain the most important event of our lives thus far and so it is vital that I do it. Abi's death has undoubtedly been the most devastating event of my life and of our family's life. Somehow we got through it; somehow we regained happiness (of sorts).

I am very aware of the huge effort I am asking of others as well as myself: that it will bring up sadness and grief; buried feelings that they may not want stirred up again; that the experience of talking again may leave them feeling upset, churned up. But our family is worth doing this for: we owe it to ourselves and to Abi. I think this will be a cathartic venture and, I hope, a positive one.

The thoughts this process has produced have led me to think that this exploration will result in further reflections about our family. What is the family? How does it exist? How do the individual members support one another? What if they can't support each other – what happens then?

A major question was, how can we, any of us, eventually feel happy and be able to laugh? One of the first things Matthew said to me after Abi died was, "I'll never be happy again". I remember saying that he would; I think I thought I could never be happy; I knew I had to help him and the other children, but I'm not sure to what extent I believed it would be possible to be happy myself. And of course, it is **possible** to be happy, but always there is a little whispered thought at the back of my mind, sometimes a feeling inside which is about Abi and the fact she isn't with us and part of the experience I or we are enjoying.

The person I am now is so different from the woman I was then. I have more confidence in myself. I am able to stand up for myself in a way that I couldn't then. I was very vulnerable; I was frozen with grief for so long and found such difficulty in relating to many people. I felt angry with myself; I didn't like myself for some of the thoughts that went through my mind.

I know I blocked my thoughts and feelings out so much over the years, but gradually more and more came out. It was so hard for me and I was able to cope with just a little at a time. I feel now I am beginning to fulfil my destiny and, at last, I have some idea about what I am here for. For many years my raison d'être has been my family; they are the most important aspect of my life and my most important achievements. We are in a new phase of life now as my children are all in their twenties and thirties.

Now that I am a granny my thoughts are changing. I know now there are people who will live beyond us. It is such a joy to me seeing children who have my genes in them, seeing the similarities to others in the family, noticing how they respond to new experiences, how they develop so fast, what they have learnt. It's hard to describe how it feels: pride, love, amazement; it's a mixture of all these feelings. It kind of calms me down and lets me think I don't need to worry about leaving a legacy behind. The grandchildren Paddy and I have are part of our legacy. Perhaps this book is the unique legacy our family owns.

In the aftermath of Abi's death I read lots of books and articles about bereavement. Many books were helpful, whilst others scared me with the facts and figures they produced (like 90% of couples split up in the wake of a child's death). But I have never read anything which focuses on the family and asks such questions as: what happens to the individuals, how do they relate to one another, what helps, what doesn't, how might someone help a person they know who has lost a child?

Each individual description the family have given of their experience is obviously a subjective one – nothing is 'right or wrong'. All responses and ways of coping are unique and they are just as they are. I realised early on that I needed to hold onto that so when someone was surprised that the children had gone to school so 'soon' afterwards, it was OK because that had been OUR decision; it was the right one for us. Sometimes it felt difficult to hold onto that feeling in the midst of what I felt (perhaps unjustly) to be criticism. No-one tells us how to behave when a child dies; we never think it will happen to us. Even if we hear about a tragedy happening to another family, we might shun it; avoid thinking about it too much. One old friend of mine told her mother when she heard the news that she thought she herself had suffered all the bad luck going around because one of her children had leukaemia as a baby. As if a jinx can only hit one person or family, and that others they know will be exempt! And for me, I thought that the loss of our stillborn daughter three years earlier was 'my lot' of tragedy. I'd had the bad times then, so nothing could strike me again.

Perhaps faith would have helped, but the only faith I had was in myself, Paddy and our children. I had a strong sense that we would be able to get through this somehow. We'd done something similar before and this was another test for us, albeit a bigger and even more devastating one. My philosophy was to get on with life.

Being bereaved is such hard work and so tiring. It felt like starting a new job: one which you didn't ask for, have had no preparation for, don't know where it's going, don't know really what you should be aiming at. Further, there is absolutely no way of going back to the old comfortable job that you could do so easily. I found I was liable to make mistakes, bumping my car through misjudging distances and trying very hard to maintain a kind of normality.

What happens more often than not is that the bereaved person has to take control, and find a way to manage others' distress at a time when they can barely function themselves. The effort of doing that is too much, but that is often how it is. As the bereaved you set the tone and the pace: others look to you to see how to behave, how to function, whether it's OK to relax, let go, laugh a little.

My own experience was that nothing really helped that much; it was only the passage of time. For me it seemed to take so long; years went by when I just existed, I lived on the periphery of my emotions and feelings. I did my best but I found it very hard to enjoy the life I had. I always wanted something more, but it was something I could never ever have.

So this book describes what happened to one ordinary family; the effect that losing our child had on the individuals involved. It is also my story: how I rose from the dead and how I left a frozen existence behind. Someone once described me as a phoenix arising from the ashes; a metaphor that stayed with me for many years. I can make the choice to arise from the ashes if I find myself down in that pit again. But I can also choose to stay there, numb and dead.

It's a place I revisit from time to time. Sometimes I have found it important to let myself descend into a dark place, to re-experience the depth of feelings I had when Abi died. It is my way of re-connecting with her, of remembering just how important she was and still is to me. I am the mother of five children, three of whom happen to be alive and well. But those other two daughters are part of me still. Just as my three living children have helped me become the woman I am now, so, too, did the two who will be forever the missing link for me.

Since it needs to be a truthful account, the feelings I had from time to time needed to be explored, faced and worked through. To a large extent I've done that with much help from many people, but there are feelings I had which I haven't said aloud. People might guess at them, that I had those feelings, but it wasn't talked about or referred to; feelings of anger, resentment, fury, despair, happiness even. Perhaps the latter is the most difficult to write about or explain. It took me years to be able to recognise that I was happy and that I was enjoying life again.

How is it I could be happy, how could I find laughter inside me? How could I enjoy life? I went through long periods of thinking that wasn't what I should do, or pretending for the sake of others' that I was happy. Inside I was still feeling numb and dead. Now I've reached the stage of describing myself (mostly) as a happy woman and it is **because** of what happened not in spite of what happened.

I have found my Self through this process. I've discovered what I have inside me: to offer help and support to others, to understand them and what they are going through, to be able to have some kind of empathy and be able to share (a little bit) the pain they are in. But I never want to give the impression that I have got 'it all sorted', that I understand and can deal with anything life throws at me. I know I have more to come, there will be more unhappiness, more times perhaps when I feel despairing again. But my guess is it will never be as bad as it was during the immediate aftermath of her death.

The children on holiday at Lindisfarne in 1984

Abi is always in my heart and I carry her with me all the time. Sometimes she is present in a very physical way, though less so now. I like to think she is with me, that she knows what I do, and that she helps me with the deeper work I do. Working through both the bereavement process and learning to work with other people in similar places, has taught me that I have a core inside me which responds to people who are deeply unhappy for a variety of reasons. Individuals don't necessarily have to be suffering from a major bereavement to be facing deep and soul-searching questions about themselves and their lives. I know that my experiences have been fundamental in enabling me to offer understanding and empathy to others.

Two

Abi's Story

Abigail Clare Neligan
Born 10th December 1981; died 16th November 1984

So what did happen...?

Abi was a beautiful baby; she was so loved and wanted by us all. We had had a stillborn daughter and the only way we could think to cope with the complete shock was to try for another baby as quickly as possible. An early miscarriage was another blow, but once the pregnancy with Abi was underway, I began to relax a little, but only a little. It was still a worrying time as she was a breech position (as all three of my daughters have been) and she was born early by elective Caesarean.

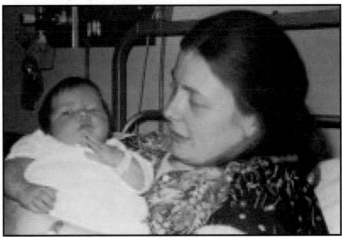

My relief to hold my new daughter
Abi, the evening she was born

It was such a magical time – a beautiful child with a beautiful name to match (Abigail means God's handmaiden). She had dark hair, long eyelashes and an easy temperament. She slotted in to our lives so easily, uncomplaining as she was dragged around in the never-ending stream of activities that her older brothers and sister were involved in. Our life was busy and it was hard work but we were all very happy. Our family was complete; we relaxed and enjoyed life a lot.

I felt I had achieved my goal at last. I had the four children I had always wanted. I loved being a Mum, creating a home, doing all the things which went along with that, such as developing my cooking skills even further, being creative and making my children those things which nowadays would probably be laughed at! We didn't have that much money, so instead of going out and buying fancy dress costumes for the children such as Superman or a nurse's outfit I set to with my sewing machine and made them. I even made Simon his much loved Superted – with his furry suit which unzipped to reveal Superted inside in all the glory of his magical blue and red suit.

We moved to Hull in early 1983 and settled in to a family house near the centre of the city. We made plenty of friends and were happy and contented, making plans for the future and hopeful for our children's futures.

By the autumn of 1984 I was feeling restless, wondering about trying to find myself some work outside the home, and the feasibility of returning to nursing. Abi was due to start nursery school very soon and I was looking forward to having some time just for me. As I look back to that time, I remember a long succession of wet days, leaves coming off the trees, the children bringing mud into the house. We must have felt restless as a family too, because we were looking at other houses, wanting to move rather than try and improve the house we were living in. Just a couple of days before she went into hospital I took her and a little friend of hers to view another house in an adjacent street. Abi wasn't well then, but it only seemed like the usual cold that children get at that time of the year, particularly with all the bugs the three other children brought into the house from school.

She spent a lot of the Monday night of that week awake and wheezing with croup. She came into our bed, so all three of us got very little sleep. We took her into the bathroom and tried to ease her croup in a steamy room, without any success. On the Tuesday morning she was tired by the lack of sleep, but nothing to make us worry significantly. She and I spent our usual sort of day: her playing with another little friend in the afternoon but she spent a lot of the day in my arms; me reading to her and trying to occupy her and keep her happy. Remembering the late afternoon and evening, it seems now not that different to any other evening. There were children to feed, homework to be supervised, Simon had a judo class, then baths for them all and get them off to bed.

When the other children come home from school, I ask Matthew, the eldest, to help get supper ready by peeling the potatoes.[1] He is standing at the kitchen sink in his school uniform, sleeves rolled up ready for his task and looking at me with an anxious expression on his face. I have Abi cradled on my right hip and tell him not to worry, "Abi isn't going to die".

Paddy comes home from work, sees she is unwell and decides we need to have her examined. He rings through

---

[1]   The rest of this chapter is written in the present tense. It is so vivid and real that it feels the only way to relate the events that followed.

to our surgery, but as soon as he hears the name of the GP who would visit, he realises that was no use as the doctor on call for the surgery wasn't someone he trusted. He decides to go right to the top and phone a colleague who is a paediatrician. She suggests we take Abi in a little later in the evening when she will be working at the nearest hospital to us in Hull. That seems reassuringly OK to us, so Paddy drives off with Simon to take him to his judo class.

I carry on with the normal routine of getting the other two children on with their homework and thinking about bedtime and what is needed for the next day. We arrange for a baby-sitter to come round while we both take her to the hospital. I get some things together to keep her happy, just in case we have to stay overnight. I take her special doll and quilt; she is wearing red pyjamas and her red dressing gown. The dressing gown is on its last legs really; all four children have worn it so it has done sterling work over the years. I wrap the quilt around her as we go out to the car and drive the short distance to the hospital. The route is well known to us; we have driven this way so many times before, it seems almost normal to be doing this. And Paddy works some of the time at this hospital so it feels quite natural in a peculiar kind of way.

Am I worried? I don't think so specially, although we have never had to do this before with any of the other children. I imagine that I think that we might have to stay overnight, but then we'll come home again and things will be fine. How is it I have no inkling of the enormity of what we are embarking on? How is it I have no sense at all that I will never be able to drive this way again, look up at the hospital without thinking about her and remembering what happened on the 13th floor?

We wait to see the doctor who is still busy with sick newborn babies in another hospital across the city. We realise even then that there aren't really enough senior staff on duty that evening. She eventually arrives and examines her. She decides what should happen. Abi and I should stay here overnight just in case something goes wrong. Abi will be in the best place to be looked after properly if she has further trouble breathing. I can see Abi is getting tired now.

Paddy goes off home to relieve our babysitter. I remember standing at the window of the ward, it is night-time now and it is very dark. Abi and I can see the car-park right down below us and we can see him striding out towards the car. He has such a distinctive walk; you couldn't mistake him for anyone else. I'm still holding her in my arms, cradled on my right hip. She waves to him and calls out, "Bye-bye, Daddy" – but he can't hear her, he's 13 floors away and on his way home to the others. He thinks she is safe and in the best possible place. That's what I think too. How wrong could we be?

She is so tired now, but I think I must keep her awake. A junior doctor is coming to put up a drip because they think she is a bit dehydrated. She decides to go to the loo, I say I'll carry her, but she insists on walking herself; she is such an independent child. We come back to the room and I sit on the bed with her on my knee. I read her stories and sing songs in an effort to keep her awake because I know the doctor will come eventually to attend to her and I don't want to have to wake her up.

Eventually a doctor and nurse come into the room to put up the drip. I'm holding Abi on my knee, holding her firm so she won't wriggle. She is sitting very still, being very good, but I know she is so tired that all she wants is to go to sleep. The doctor is very young; he is having trouble putting up the drip. He can't get the needle into a vein; he is trying to put it into her foot. Suddenly the nurse, who has been standing behind me, asks Abi if she is all right. They both look at her, they begin to shake her arm, she doesn't respond. Suddenly she is pulled from my arms, more nurses come into the room, one of them takes me away. I find myself sitting out on the landing beside the lifts. It is very bright out there, and there are a lot of lights burning. There are windows all around, it's still so very dark outside but I don't know what time it is.

Somehow I've rung Paddy, I've told him he must come **now**, Abi's heart has stopped. Now I don't know how I knew that. I just need him here with me. I need her with me too. I am waiting. It feels like forever, and yet it feels like no time. The lift stops, Paddy rushes out towards me. How did he get here so quickly, who is looking after the other children? We cling to one another; there doesn't seem anything to say. Paddy asks me what has happened, I tell him what little I know. I think the nurse who was with me has gone now. We seem to be on our own. A doctor comes past, but he doesn't look at us or meet our eyes. Paddy knows he is part of the resuscitation team. We are still waiting.

Then I feel something releases inside me, something drops inside me. I turn to him and say, "I think she just died". Paddy says, "You felt it too?" There is such a sense of silence inside my body, I feel like I am in a bubble of some kind. I think that was my first experience of letting the transpersonal[2] tell me what was happening, rather than me working it out in my head. I *felt* something; deep inside me and I had a complete knowledge of what it

---

[2]   Transpersonal: relating to states or areas of consciousness beyond the limits of personal identity.

was. It was something I couldn't ignore or pretend wasn't there.

Thinking more about this experience it feels like I was fully aware for the first time of something bigger than me, feeling a connection so visceral it overwhelmed me. I had the sensation of feeling the connection with Abi so deeply and somehow at the same time that connection was severed completely. No part of my being was unaffected: I had the physical connection, the mental awareness of what had happened and a spiritual 'knowing' that she had died. In that moment Abi had left us.

But also I had the questioning inside my head. This is not happening to us; this cannot be happening to us; this cannot be true. It reminded me of the feelings I had after giving birth: the physical fullness disappearing in an instance, but the connection still there with the child who is now in the world; the peculiar sensation inside whilst my body re-acclimatised to the new reality.

Within a few minutes the same doctor who couldn't look us in the eyes returns and says they are taking Abi to Intensive Care. Things looked bad when he arrived, but they have got her breathing again. So perhaps I was wrong? She didn't die?

I don't know how I get to ICU but I find myself beside her bed, she is a tiny little figure on a big high bed, surrounded by tubes, a ventilator breathing for her. This is a surreal experience. I don't know what happens next. There are three long days and nights to live through. Three days and nights in which I spend all my time with her, either sitting with my head beside her, weeping into the sheets or holding her on my knee so I can cuddle her. It's like being in suspended animation. I know in my heart what is going to happen in the end. I know deep down it has already happened. Abi died when I was sitting out on that landing.

We all have to somehow get through these next three days and nights until the medical team catches up with what has already happened and tell us what we already know. Abi has gone. At this stage though, I don't know how long I will have to go with this agony of watching her leave us in imperceptibly small steps.

It is the longest time of my life, longer than the hours I spent giving birth to any of the children. I don't leave the hospital; I don't want to eat; I just want this nightmare to end. But I cannot bear the idea of her dying and not being here in my life. No matter how bad it feels, at least she is warm on my knee and in my arms. There is something of Abi there, even if her essence has gone.

The other children come in to visit her, at first just to see her, but later on to say goodbye. My mother comes down from Newcastle to help look after the children at home, then Paddy's mother and my father arrive. Our closest friends come to say goodbye to Abi.

The eczema she suffered from since being a small baby has disappeared due to the strong steroids she is being given. Her skin looks beautifully smooth, her blonde hair feathers around her face. I hold her hand, I stroke her. I care for her. I can do that instead of the nurses. Adrian, our next-door neighbour, who happens to be a vicar visits. I don't want to see him – what can God do for me or Abi now? It's a waste of my time to talk to him; I need to be with her all the time. My sleeping is a waste of time, so I refuse to sleep. I will not leave her. She has her special doll on her bed. Her quilt which she loved covers her. Some of the children's friends have made get well cards for her – they are decorating her room in intensive care. Those children think she will be back home soon, a little bit weak but she will be playing with them again in a while. It is not going to happen.

Paddy insists we leave the room and go down to the hospital canteen for a drink and something to eat. It's a soulless place, bright lights again, full of people talking, laughing, whilst we are talking about offering her organs for donation. It feels surreal. We have this most desperate, appalling decision to make – perhaps we look normal to other people; perhaps they have the same kind of agony as we do. But where do you go to talk about things like that? It's like the most impossible thing I could imagine is juxtaposed with the most normal everyday experience – buying a cup of tea and a sandwich. We decide we'll suggest transplantation to the doctors: something good must come out of this.

We know she is going to die, that it is only a matter of time. We are desperately trying to think of something positive. It's better that Abi dies than she survives but with brain-damage. She was so bright; she was so intelligent; she would have achieved so much in her life. We couldn't cope with her being a vegetable. We can have happy memories of her. How did we have the strength to think that then?

She has been down to theatre for the pressure to be relieved on her brain. The nurses cut off some of her hair where the drill had to go into her skull. I thank them; it was thoughtful of them. It's in an envelope with her name on so I can keep it safe. Maybe my mother, and the children, will like to have some of her hair later. The operation doesn't do anything. What was the point of putting her through that? Did she know anything about it?

We know time is running out. Paddy insists on going in with the doctors who are performing the brain-death tests. He wants to make 100% sure the tests are done in the right way; that there can be no possible question about the outcome. I can't imagine how he has the strength to do that – is he being a father or a doctor then? What is he feeling? I think he is doing this for all of us; putting himself through this utmost test of his resilience.

The rest of us, the children and Abi's grandparents, are all sitting in a room together. The neurosurgeon and Paddy come into the room. The doctor tells us that Abi has died. There is no more hope. It is over. There are tears. I have never seen my father cry before.

Paddy and I go back to say our last goodbyes. Everyone else has gone home. We take more of her hair and kiss her. I worry – we have donated her organs but I don't want to see her after that has happened. Her eyes were so beautiful; I can't bear to think about them being removed.   She has such a lovely little body, I know it was the right decision but the thought of her body being mutilated and damaged is something else I can't bear. I push the images away.

I pick up her quilt and her doll, her dressing gown and her pyjamas. Her pyjamas were cut up the side so the doctors could work on her. What a shame, they were lovely pyjamas. I cuddle them all as we walk out to the lift. I really am leaving her here on her own. I am going away from her. I feel I have abandoned her. I don't think then what I think later: that she has abandoned us; she has left us without saying goodbye. If I could have said goodbye to her, what would I have said? How would I have told her what she meant to me? How would I prepare her for what is coming next? I never thought this would happen.

We walk out into the night, to find the car. I think my father is with us. It is very quiet; I don't think we speak much. I get in the car. In the middle of the back of our car is her child-seat. She'll never sit in it again, waving to friends as we drive past them, shouting to her brothers and sister, singing songs, crying because she wants to get out of her seat and I won't let her.

We drive home. It is as quick as the drive when we took her in to the hospital just four days ago. Our whole lives have changed. What do we do now? How can I manage? How will I live?

Three

The Aftermath

There are so many questions about what happened. The simple truth as we later worked it out was that the doctor was inexperienced and couldn't do what was needed in the emergency that arose, and the resuscitation team took too long to get there. So her life ended in a few minutes.

I never ever thought I would have to plan a funeral for one of my children. What I wanted was to get the whole episode over as quickly as possible, so in fact I never gave myself time to think about the best way to celebrate her life, what the options were. I realise now that I became a block; without real feelings because if I allowed myself to have the feelings I would fall apart. It was important that I continued to look after the family in the best way I could, that was my priority. I thought I was feeling: I knew I was crying; I knew I was feeling physical pain when the truth dawned on me every morning as I faced another day to struggle through. I wonder what it would have been like to really feel, to really experience, to let everything else drift on whilst I lay, or sat, or walked, and let the feelings wash over me.

I know some cultures encourage the bereaved to do just that, so they have a specific period of time when they have no duties in the community and can just let the feelings out. There was a kind of feeling of contamination, I was having thoughts and feelings I had never had before. I wanted something very awful to happen to those who were involved in her 'care', those were feelings that were alien to me. I didn't like those thoughts at all, so I tried to push them away, bury them. I wonder if a more healthy response would have been to allow them to surface, express them so that they didn't hold a magical intensity. I would have needed someone very strong with me to help me go through that, and the strong person I had, who I relied on utterly, who I think would have understood and allowed me the freedom to express that, was suffering himself.

The question 'why' cropped up time after time – why me, why us, why her, why now? We never found an answer to those questions – apart from why not? The platitude some people offered us that 'God' only gives those people the challenges to face that they can cope with seemed unhelpful in the extreme. People said things like, "No-one should have to bury their child, no-one should see their child die before they do". Maybe not, but for some of us that is the reality and we need to find a way to go through it.

I had times of feeling I was going mad with grief, feeling I was different from everyone else, I thought, "I should be over it by now". I became very intolerant, judgemental and caustic in my thoughts about what I perceived to be thoughtless suggestions by others. It is only with time that I learned to be more gentle and understanding of myself and others. I realised that very few people had direct experience of the situation we had found ourselves in and if they made a suggestion it was with the best of motives. Now I know that it takes as long as it takes. But that is all I know. What happens in you and to you is right for you. What you feel like doing is right for you.

Virtually the moment we returned home after Abi died, we began to think about what we wanted to do for her.

We decided to have a very small funeral with just the family, but to have a 'celebration of her life' meeting[3] at our home a little later so that all our friends and their children could attend.

There were so many decisions and things to think about yet I found it impossible to make decisions – my brain was feeling like cotton-wool and I felt unable to have any kind of clarity. I remember I had to explain to the hairdresser what had happened, why I was so pale and quiet when I went to have my hair cut before the meeting to celebrate her life.

We chose Saturday 24th November as the day, and it dawned very bright. I realised what a lot of strength our friends and family had and how they were willing their love and support towards us all. People were coming from around the country to be with us all that day. I had asked my friends in Hull to make cakes and we had all those laid out for afterwards. We had put photos around the house showing the happy times we had all had with Abi.

We waited for some friends to arrive who were coming up from Birmingham but in the end we had to start before they got there. This was a week after Abi died, the weather had changed and it was a crisp, sunny day with the sun streaming in the windows. There were crowds of people in our sitting room, lots of children there and people sitting on the floor, anywhere they could park themselves.

---

[3] Paddy and I originally met as teenagers through Quakers and, to some extent, our early 'courtship' was witnessed by the Quaker Meeting in Newcastle. We had a Quaker wedding and many of the values and principles held by Quakers are still important to us.

If your partner or parent dies, the chances are that you have talked over the years and have an idea about what kind of funeral to have, how to celebrate their life and so on. When your little child dies, you have no idea. It seemed that people wanted us to make decisions quickly, to get on with it and get it over with. Almost like, once it is over everyone can return to normal life and things will be OK again. As if! And of course, from other people's perspectives, they do want you to make decisions: they don't want to have to think it through with you; they don't want to face the truth that you are attempting to assimilate. They want to get whatever it is over with and get back to their normal life and try to forget about the agony you are going through.

In many ways, things got even harder after the funeral and the meeting of celebration. I had long nights of tossing and turning, which then led into a long-term sleeping difficulty. I used to walk round the house, looking at photos, drinking cups of tea at the kitchen table in the middle of the night – the quiet, still house. That's one of the things I remember: that from being a noisy house, always seeming to be full of children playing, laughing, talking and fighting, it suddenly all went so quiet. The children were asked out; we had kind friends who wanted to do something for them and me. But we didn't ask people back, I didn't know how to be around other children any more. I felt awkward and uncomfortable. The house seemed so empty all of a sudden. How could one small child have that effect so quickly? What a stamp she made in her almost three years on this earth.

There were things that happened to us which we could never have predicted and we had to find our ways of dealing with those awkward situations. Someone said to us, "But no-one dies of croup!" I can remember my feelings then: wanting to scream at her, "How can you be so insensitive and stupid? **Our** child has died!" In reality, I was very polite.

After Abi had died but before the news got round to everyone we knew, we felt that people were still avoiding us (not a lot, but it did happen) just because they didn't know what to say. They knew she was very ill, but didn't want to ask questions of us. Other people asked in a bright and breezy way: so how is she now? It was all so hard to cope with, but the kind of thing that happens to many people in similar circumstances.

I remember that I had to take some new items of clothing back to Mothercare because Abi had died and I no longer had need of the clothes. I had to explain why I was returning the clothes because the receipt had gone missing. I sat and waited for the assistant to return, feeling like there was a peculiar space around me, thinking they were talking about me and they weren't sure what approach to take. I felt so COLD; felt so scared. What if they didn't believe me and I had to argue it out? How could I do that? How could I prove my child had died and so I had no need of those clothes? In the end, I didn't need to and I guess just one look at me was enough to prove I was telling the truth.

I hadn't thought about why I needed to take those clothes back at all until Cathy asked me when she was reading a first copy of this book. We talked about it and I suspect I needed to put myself through it because it was another way of making what had happened become real to myself. For much of the time soon after Abi died, I felt like I was walking around in a bubble, nothing was connecting with me; life didn't seem real at all. Every morning when I woke up, the reality of Abi's death would hit me all over again. Paddy had been so wonderful in telling people, writing letters and so on and I hadn't had to tell anyone really. That trip into Mothercare with a snowsuit intended for the winter which was no longer needed was, I think, my way of beginning to imprint into myself the fact that she wasn't alive any more and she never would be. At no point did I think about giving it to someone else, asking a friend to return it for me, throwing it away, or giving it to a charity shop.

I remember we received appointments for her next set of immunisations through the post several months after her death. I wondered why there isn't a way of avoiding that kind of painful intrusion. I had the sense that because I had had this huge change to my life, the whole world should have known about it and be sensitive to me. How could anyone NOT know what had happened?

Sometimes I would avoid other people myself. I would spot friends or acquaintances as I drove my car (which was very distinctive, no-one could pretend they hadn't seen me driving it) and I would pretend I hadn't seen them. Sometimes I wouldn't answer the door when friends came round; I was unable to cope with any more sympathy. I would occasionally find myself crawling around on the floor in case someone caught sight of me through the window. I found it so difficult to say, "Not now, but please can you come back another time". I just could not do that.

I found a way to fool the social worker who had been recommended to us by the hospital consultant who counselled me for a while that I was actually all right and I was coping and managing life well enough. Looking back, I did a good acting job there. I almost fooled myself too!

That social worker said one thing to me that really stuck, which was that I would be the anchor. Other people would look to me for how to behave and what to say. It might seem as if that was the last thing I would need, but that would happen. And she was right. I was incredulous when she brought it up, but it happened over and over again. Maybe that is how it should be, that those supportive people around the bereaved do need to take their lead from the key individuals, but it requires so much strength. And perhaps friends and family need to learn how to ask questions which allow an opening into sharing, an opening into closure.

We spent years with Abi's toys around, with her clothes tucked away and not able to move on. Eventually we moved house. That was painful but felt like the right decision when we finally did make the move and I had times of wondering if we should have moved earlier and made ourselves do it. We moved out of the city five years before we finally left Hull but that felt like an interim phase. I think we wanted to see if we could manage it, although the spoken reason for moving out of Hull was in order to give me more opportunities to expand and develop my work. Looking back it was a stepping-stone to leaving the city and leaving Abi behind. When we finally moved away from Hull I was so relieved and I realised I had been ready to move right away several years before.

I went through long spells of thinking that there was nothing I could say to my children which was the truth because the fundamental responsibility of my role as a mother, of looking after them and caring for them no matter what it took, had been shattered. I hadn't managed to protect Abi and she had died. That was something I had done to them. Those were thoughts I had for a long time, and I took the responsibility and the blame. It took me many years to see that this was something that had happened, and I and we had to learn to live with it.

Abi dying wasn't my fault, and it wasn't Paddy's fault. And I needn't blame others either, not when they didn't make this situation happen. It wasn't their fault either. People did the best they could but their best just wasn't good enough. And even though it happened to Abi, it could still happen again to another child, another baby, if the support for the medical staff wasn't there. This isn't a tirade against them; it is really hard being part of the medical profession, knowing what goes on from the 'other side of the bed'. There was a part of Paddy and me that wanted to support them, but how could we do that, when our child had died?

I have remembered one or two vivid memories that I had blotted out. I always used to lay the breakfast table the evening before to save precious time in the morning. A couple of days after she died I unconsciously laid her place too with her special bowl and mug. It was heartbreaking to pick them up off the table and put them back into the cupboard.

Another memory I have is of hoping and praying that the hospital would find they had made a mistake and they would bring her home to us. I visualised her in someone's arms, ringing our front door bell and when I went to answer it there she would be, smiling at me and happy to see me. That memory is one that went on for a long time and is one I kept to myself. It felt so real, the picture in my mind of her beyond the glass with a broad smile on her face, as if she had been teasing me with her absence. When those longings came into my mind, a part of me thought, "Maybe I'm a little bit mad here, maybe I had better not tell anyone about this".

That re-stimulation of the intense grief happened over and over again in unexpected ways. The triggers lessened over the years, but could still rise up again and hit me with huge force when I least expected it. Gradually I began to understand that I was able to weather the feelings; they would eventually abate and I would feel more in control of myself.

Other questions were alive too. What effect did the way Abi died have, for example, on the young doctor who tried, and failed, to put up a drip, during which procedure she went into respiratory arrest? When did he realise he didn't know what to do, that things had gone badly wrong, that this was a child who was dying in front of him? He would have known that any help would take some time to get there, he needed to be sure of what to do, to get on and do it. But he tried and didn't do it well enough. He has had that experience to live with for the last twenty years.

I feel sympathy for him now, and I'm letting myself think about him rather than blocking it out. To be unsupported, to know there was no-one around for him to call on and to watch a child die in front of him must have been a terrible experience. My guess is that it affected him through his career and I wonder what he does now. Knowing that doctors don't forget those traumatic experiences doesn't help me. It hasn't helped me over the years to wonder how he might have dealt with a child of his own who had croup, or cared for another child in hospital with a similar condition. I hope he learnt from it and that it made him a better doctor. Perhaps he was more able to ask for help, and be less willing to be left alone when he felt inexperienced as well as more able to empathise with patients and parents. Who knows.

I have thought about contacting the consultant who looked after Abi in hospital and finding out what the experience was like for her. There was a personal link (because her husband was a colleague of Paddy's) and I assume that must have made it hard for her. After Abi died, she suggested we sue the Health Authority, but our feeling was that the only people it would really hurt would be ourselves. I wonder what effect Abi's death had on her, but she and her husband eventually left Hull and we lost touch.

When I thought about this more deeply I realised there is a part of me that is protecting her. If I never contact her I won't have to put her through the thoughts and feelings about the decisions she made at the time. At the time I thought I was the one with the problem (which of course I was) and that I should be able to be an adult and entertain her in my home along with other colleagues of Paddy's. I look back now and think this was madness. How could I be expected, and expect myself, to rise above that – to put my feelings aside and bury them in order to be welcoming and warm to a woman who had done the unthinkable: she had let my child die.

Part of my struggle over the years was that very thought in relation to myself. **I was the woman who had done that unthinkable thing: I had let my child die.** I was there with Abi; I had not protected my daughter. I should have known what was happening. I should have had that sixth sense that something was going badly wrong. I should have demanded help earlier. I should have done what no-one else could do. In other words I should have been Superwoman. But I wasn't. I was me. And that has been the huge realisation I have had to come to terms with, to challenge my thoughts about myself as a woman and a mother over the years since Abi died.

Deep down I know there is a part of me, a shadow side, that I don't like, which wants to punish that consultant. I want her to understand how difficult it has been, how destructive to each one of us, that we have each had so many problems in different ways which have originated in that tremendous loss. It was so hard to come to terms with the fact that I needed to stop punishing myself; no matter what I did, no punishment to myself was going to bring Abi back and I owed it to myself, Paddy and the family to learn how to live again and to move on. I had to find a way through, I needed to learn how to find happiness in my life. I had to find fulfilment for myself. No-one else could do that for me, no matter how much they might have wanted to take the pain away. That was an impossible task for anyone.

Paddy gave himself torture afterwards, thinking that if Abi had been at home and she had stopped breathing as she did in hospital he could have saved her by doing a tracheotomy. Would he really have been able to do that?

Those thoughts lead into Paddy's story and the conversation we had...

Four

Paddy

Paddy and I have been together since we were in our teens and so have literally grown up together; learning about ourselves and one another along the way. We have created a family together, made several comfortable homes and supported one another during our lives and the challenges we faced. We have both changed, as would be expected. When I first knew him, he was a shy teenager who was having difficulties with his relationship with his father. I believe I gave him confidence in himself, helped him become more articulate and assertive and have a belief in himself. In turn he helped me to have the kind of life I wanted: he supported me and understood that it was important for me to be at home with my children as they grew and developed. I was very fortunate that we were able to make those choices, and I often think how lucky I was that he thought it was as important as I did, and that we had the means to be able to do that, even though at times it was a financial struggle.

Paddy went through medical school whilst I trained as a nurse. We were studying in different parts of the country during this time which put a strain on our relationship, but we weathered it and we married six months before he qualified as a doctor. We then spent several years moving round the country as he pursued his career and decided what he wanted to specialise in. This meant that I organised house moves, new schools, created new networks for us to be involved with and made new friends in new towns. Paddy is a very conscientious, focussed

35

person; his work has always been very important to him and he gave 100% to his patients and his work commitments.

It took me a long time to get round to talking to Paddy for the purposes of this book. Partly I think this was because I felt we have talked so much over the years about what it all meant, how we felt, how we could move forward and what we needed to do. I thought I knew most of his feelings and thoughts and wondered what new insights there could be. With the rest of the family, I had a strong sense of wanting to know what it was like for them but I felt I knew a lot of Paddy's experience. That doesn't mean that sometimes over the years it hasn't been hard to talk to each other: particularly I think when either one of us seemed to be 'coping better' than the other. I

Paddy's birthday, 4th July 1984:
Abi is looking forward to tucking
into strawberries and cream

remember I used to feel resentful at times because Paddy seemed able to move on 'faster' than I did, he had his work as a focus and appeared to be functioning 'normally'. I felt stuck in grief for many years and found it hard to move on.

Writing this has brought Abi back to us in a new way. Paddy and I have discussed the book's longer-term implications, for us and the family. I remember him saying at one point, when I think I was being particularly excited and enthusiastic about what it could all mean that he didn't want me to forget that she was his daughter too. That remark brought me up short. This book was my idea, I had the impetus and urge to write and was very involved in thinking about how to approach the whole project.

Not long after she died he'd said that he wanted to write something about her, but it never happened. I didn't want to steal anything from him, this is my story but perhaps Paddy has his own story to tell. Or perhaps his story will be told through this too.

I felt very close to him as we got into our conversation, and I remembered that in the past when we talked about Abi it brought us very close together because of the shared pain and distress. So Paddy and I talked on a bright sunny day in our sitting room.

As a place to start I asked what were his strongest memories of that time.

"There is just so much; days and days worth of memories. A lot of the memories of the time when she was unwell at home are about feeling guilty: why didn't I do that; why did I do this and so on. Why did I take Simon to judo that

evening? I just don't understand that. Judo doesn't matter. I didn't realise the importance of what was happening.

Some strong, strong memories I have are of when we took her into the hospital; in our arms, in your arms, in my arms. What she said then: 'I wish the doctor would hurry up', something like that. She was completely herself. Even though she was struggling with her breathing, she was still her. The essence of her was still there. And the power of that. I've never thought of it this way before, but it's just come to me that she thought the world revolved around her. And of course it did because she wasn't even three.

I already had feelings of irritation with the medical staff before anything went wrong. There had been a sort of reassurance in getting in to the hospital because I'd been worrying all evening about whether she needed to be in hospital or not. So when Elspeth said, yes she does need to because we may need to do this and that, I felt reassured. Even though she, Elspeth, needed to go off to another hospital, we could leave it to her clinical experience and she would make the necessary decisions. So I must have felt relieved then and felt it was OK to go back home to sort the children out.

Then having gone home and got the children to bed, that phone call from you which was just... devastating, stunning. I just went into a sort of automatic routine: this is what I need to do and I got on and did it. I got hold of Chris[4] then I jumped into the car and drove to the hospital talking out loud to Abi."

Do you remember what you were saying?

---

[4]   Maggie and Chris were our closest friends in Hull. Chris came to babysit.

38

"You'd used the phrase 'her heart has stopped'. I was saying something like 'start up again, start up again, start up again...' as I was driving. As I recall, you were already out on the landing when I got up there.

We were just holding each other. Feeling desperate. Wanting to know what was happening. We couldn't do anything. Then I don't know if I had it then or if you told me about it later – this feeling that something had happened, like a switch.

I remember the sheepish doctor who walked past us. I can't remember how Abi got down to intensive care. Her heart was going again, so I thought it was just a matter of her being ventilated for a little while."

So you thought that, in spite of the feeling of the 'switch'? We did talk about it, I said I think something has happened, I think she's died, that's what I said and you said you felt it too.

"Yes, I thought that, despite the feeling that something devastating had happened. But then we were told her heart had started. Someone said, 'It didn't look good when we got here, but we've got her back'. Someone else talked to us at some stage, he was a Senior Registrar who said there was a problem: the tube in her throat was misplaced, so he replaced it and her heart started again. And I still thought it was just a question of her recovering.

Then we talked later on to Elspeth who was much more cagey about it. I think I suddenly realised she was being very cagey, and that's when I started to fear that Abi might be brain-damaged. The next few days just blur into one – though not quite that because I did have to keep on going home to sort out the children. I don't think you ever came home did you?"

No.

"I felt absolutely stripped. At first I had a feeling there was a bit of hope, in the early stage a lot of hope and some fear. What happened was that the fear got more and more, and the hope got less and less. There was a chilling moment when I was at home, I don't know which day it was, when our friend Lesley came round with cards for Abi from her children. She asked when Abi would be home and I said I don't think she will be coming home. Brutal – the brutality was intended for me, not Lesley, but of course she got the force of it. I was really confronting it for myself. I remember this awful image of Abigail being mentally damaged, being physically handicapped."

(Paddy was deep in his thoughts at this point and seemed oblivious to me being there and anything I said. He began to tell me about a past experience he had had as a medical student, which had clearly stayed with him and affected him deeply.)

"I had been involved with a child who had a respiratory arrest and suffered anoxic brain damage. When I went back to the ward well over a year later as a houseman, the little boy was still on the unit – it was just awful. The picture I had was of Abi getting bigger and bigger and being physically helpless. I realised that was actually worse than her dying, and that she was going to die. I think it would have been very selfish to want her to live like that."

Do you remember much about talking to the other children?

"As I remember, I didn't tell the children I was going to the hospital; Chris just came round to stay in the house with

them. When I went back in the early hours of the morning, they were still asleep. I can't remember what I said in the morning, I think they went off to school; I think I took them to school. I must have told them she was very poorly. I'm sure I didn't tell them at that stage that she was going to die; I don't think I knew that then."

I guess you wouldn't have sent them off to school having told them that anyway.

"No, I remember them being upset but I can't remember the detail. I remember Cathy crying. Of course there was this business of having just re-arranged the bedrooms and putting the girls in together. They just had one night together, then Abi had one night in our bed and then she was in hospital.

We spent what seemed like an endless time in the hospital. We sat in the soulless hospital canteen, and watched people coming and going. We must have talked about things then: what might happen to her; whether she would live or die; what we might be dealing with in the future if she did live. The canteen was the place that we began to think that we should offer her organs for transplantation. The idea came from us, rather than any medical staff bringing up the possibility. It felt an inappropriate place to be talking about transplants.

I remember feeling that nothing was too much trouble for the nurses, whatever we wanted or needed, they tried to give us. All we really wanted was privacy with Abi. I had that feeling of holding each other all the time, though I'm sure we didn't. Feeling we were locked together."

I remember holding her on my knee a bit later on when my mother brought the children in to see her.

"That's when we knew she was dying."

One thing I recall is that you were protecting me from everything, or the facts anyway or you would interpret the facts for me. You went and had conversations with doctors which I didn't but you insisted on being there.

"I wanted to know what they could do, what they were going to do, what they were thinking. They didn't know where to put themselves of course."

Were you veering between being a father and a doctor?

"Very strikingly: I was only a doctor once. After the ventilator was switched off, I insisted it should be turned on again to preserve the organs for transplant. That was after her brain death tests. Perhaps that was being an informed father not a doctor. I wanted to see the tests; I wanted it

Paddy's love and pride in Abi

absolutely confirmed. I couldn't have taken it from someone telling me. I remember being obsessed with the machines; the intra-cranial pressure monitor – just looking at it.

I can't remember the actual moment when I knew she was going to die. I have strong feelings and memories about before and after, but I can't get the actual moment.

I haven't remembered this for a long time but when she was alive and well I loved her with a real intensity that sometimes manifested as a pain in my chest. I remember seeing her lying in her bed asleep – her long dark eyelashes on her cheeks, those rosy cheeks and her rather big lips. Just that pain. At the time it was a happy pain, but now it's a terrible pain, it hurts.

All that time the rest of the world was completely suspended. What happened to day or night? There must have been some reference to time, keeping in touch with what was happening at home. Did your mother take the children to school?"

I think you did – they didn't go to school on the Friday – I can't remember about the Thursday.

"Did they come in to the hospital on the Thursday?"

They came in twice. On the Friday we were all there in the room when the neurosurgeon came into the room and told us that she had died.

"Wasn't I with him then?"

Yes, we were all waiting and you were with him. Simon was the only one of the children to have a strong memory of that. It made a real impression on him that his remark had been at first addressed to the children – describing that it was their sister who had died rather than our daughter. I don't know how intentional this was, but I think it helped Simon at the time. He felt accounted for, that he was important and that their relationship of sisters and brothers was important.

"After that the grandparents took the kids home and you and I went back in to say goodbye to her."

We cut off some more of her hair then to take home with us.

"We had a continuing tension between hope and despair right through that time. Part of my brain was separate from the rest – the logical reasoning part of my brain was still running round, doing that thing that it does so well. I don't know how logical it really was. I was thinking about the technical aspects of things: if that's happening then that means this; if this is happening it means something else. I suppose it's that the thinking part is separate from the feeling part."

There's safety in the thinking part because the feeling part would be overwhelming. Knowing you, a large part was also wanting to protect me, the children, everyone.

"I couldn't..."

(As he said this, I heard again the despair in his voice.)

I can remember you saying that I had to have something to eat, or get some sleep, though I didn't want to, I didn't want to leave her for a moment, just in case something happened and I wasn't there with her. I'm not sure, looking back, that I was frightened she would die and I wasn't there, or that suddenly a miracle might happen, she might just wake up and be herself again and I wanted to be there for that.

"You were in such terrible pain. I couldn't protect you from it, so I had to do something."

Adrian came in – do you remember?

"I'd forgotten that.   The person visiting I remember most is my mother – who was distraught in a way I'd never seen before. It wasn't that florid, but I guess she wanted to protect me.

Abi had cut her head 10 days earlier.   I was so glad we hadn't taken her in to hospital to get it stitched up, because we would have put her through that trauma for no reason."

I don't remember that at all. It's surprised me how much I have forgotten, or pushed out of my memory.

I remember how angry you were with Elspeth when we met her. Perhaps it wasn't with her, but it was directed at her because she was the only other person in the room. Did the anger come then, or were you feeling angry before that point?

"Interesting you say about the time delay; I can remember not being angry.   It was almost a conscious decision to not be angry with some of the things that the junior doctor had done.   One turning point was possibly that I, or rather we, got a letter from the District General manager at the hospital. I wrote back to him. After I'd done that, I realised I was angry with the authorities and the system.   That echoes my mother's anger when my father died – he'd given so much to the Health Service and it let him down because it didn't save him. The Health Service let us down too, not through a lack of knowledge or an inability to treat Abi but because of pathetically inadequate staffing.   Elspeth was a locum consultant trying to cover two hospitals at once with one very junior doctor at each and no middle grade doctor at all."

She made the decision to leave one hospital and go to another and leave Abi with an inexperienced doctor.

"I don't remember any conscious thinking about that part of it, but it did occur to me on some level. If she had stayed till Abi had a drip up, what would have happened? But why did she need a drip anyway? What if Elspeth had been able to stay – and the crucial thing here is that she decided not to stay. It was her decision to choose the most important thing to do and she got it wrong."

Of course you didn't know what was going to happen and children do deteriorate very quickly.

"And because children do go off quickly, that is the very reason why you need someone competent to deal with it, there on the spot and not in another hospital across town."

So it sounds like actually you were angry with Elspeth – she was symbolic of the system and the authorities and she had made that decision.

"She was in an impossible position."

Did it make it worse, that she was John's[5] wife?

"It made it more difficult to be angry with her. I think even if I hadn't known her at all I would have found it very hard to accuse her of doing anything wrong, because I have made wrong decisions too; the best decision I could at the time with the information in front of me, but wrong. If she had stayed and Abi had been OK, the baby at the maternity hospital might have died."

---

[5]   John was one of Paddy's colleagues.

We made our decisions too – like taking Si to judo and not getting the GP out.

"That's another bit of my anger with the General Practice. I can't remember at what stage I phoned the GP and I got transferred through to the emergency doctor. When I was told who was on call, I felt it wasn't worth having them out. I didn't trust their knowledge or experience. I suppose that nearly always when I am angry it's with me as well as with others. We perhaps should have called the doctor first thing that morning."

She wasn't that ill; we'd had the children being poorly like that before and not called the doctor.

(As we were talking I realised we were in a typical discussion between the two of us. I was trying to make things all right while Paddy was working out what really happened. He was quite emphatic as he talked and explained his thinking to me.)

"She was that ill, because she died later on that day. That's not true though: although her croup was still going on after so long, she wasn't really bad at this stage. We had had two bad nights and croup shouldn't go on that long, but that's the huge benefit of hindsight, and that's why we should have called the doctor in the morning, but what a doctor would have done is quite another matter. I don't think she died of croup; it was because she had croup that they put the drip up. Then her heart stopped when the needle was put in her arm – and then incompetent resuscitation compounded it. If we hadn't taken her to hospital, she might still be alive. I don't know when I developed that thinking. I certainly didn't discuss it with you at the time. I can remember I read years later about

not putting needles into children with croup for that very reason, which confirmed what I had always feared.

Coming back to my anger with Elspeth, I think what she said about why Abi died was true as far as it went, but it didn't describe the cause of death. I needed to know that. I don't think a lot of doctors have my drive to explain. They are quite content to put down bronchopneumonia as a cause of death for a patient – but although bronchopneumonia may be present it does not necessarily adequately explain what happened."

Do you think getting your anger out helped?

"The thing I can most remember from that meeting is of her saying, 'Why don't you sue the Health Authorities?' I thought the damage it would do would be far more than any conceivable gain. Damage to us as well as to anyone involved. I had a recognition that we just needed to accept what had happened."

Did you ever feel like giving up medicine?

"NO".

(He said this very firmly.)

"I think, if anything, it made me want to be a better doctor and it did do that. I became much more sensitive to the feelings of people who were dying, both patients and relatives of those with life threatening illness."

I suppose it helped with all the work you did later in teaching junior doctors; the breaking bad news work-shops and all that kind of communication?

"That's right. A few years later I was on a working party on the care of the dying. The experience of Abi dying greatly coloured my approach to that work."

Just going back, after she died we went home. The house was full of people. My parents, your mother, the kids...

"The moment you said that about the house being full, my head was saying the house was empty. I guess that is what I felt like – I was empty. We brought her doll, 'Crybaby', home. I can't remember getting home. I can just remember going out of the hospital after she died. I remember that feeling of seeing other people, going around and getting on with their lives.

I suppose you're right, the house must have been full. And I suppose we started making plans for what to do. Lots of people came round over the weekend; calling on us. Ginna came. I remember Martin and Sarah most of all, maybe because mainly the women came and Martin was one of the rare men. They brought stuff for us to eat and so on.

Someone from the undertakers came round, it seems we held onto things we were focussed on – choosing some music, what to say, the announcement in the newspaper. The fact we wanted to celebrate her life. 'Whoever cared about Abi... is welcome' – that was the phrase we used.

We must have told other people. I have no recollection of needing to tell people, everyone just seemed to know via the grapevine."

Can you remember much about her funeral?

"We decided we were only having family and very close friends."

It was only family – not even Maggie and Chris.

"Her little coffin felt all wrong. The funeral wasn't how I wanted it. We should have taken her in our car from our house. It was impersonal; maybe us taking her would have made a difference. We did what I thought was best."

One thing was that we had to make the major decisions too quickly, and we had no guidance.

"The undertaker was very helpful and we just agreed to what he suggested."

We didn't take the time to make our own decisions. We could have asked others for help, like our parents.

"In retrospect, we should have done. The undertaker came so quickly, he was there the day afterwards. If we could have waited a couple more days... but I guess we wanted to get on and get it sorted. I think I felt the actual cremation was less important than celebrating her life. Which is true. I'd forgotten that they played the wrong music at her funeral – they played the movement before the one we wanted, though it's hard to separate them. But we didn't say anything. There was no kind of service. We decided to do it that way and it seemed like the right thing at the time."

It wasn't Abi though, was it?

"We both had an idea of what we wanted for the meeting on the Saturday afterwards. It was hard to explain it or describe it. I think it was easier to say what we didn't want rather than what we did. I wanted people to be there. We wanted children there. We wanted to affirm her, how wonderful she was and how important those three

years were. Even then, however hard it was, I wanted to recognise it was much more important that she had lived than she had died. I wouldn't have been without those three years.

I don't have the faintest idea what I said. I can remember carefully planning it to the extent that I remember we had asked Adrian to help as I was seriously concerned I wouldn't be able to speak. If that happened I wanted him to take over so I had to explain to him what I wanted to say. This is terrible but I can't remember if you spoke? I think you wanted to but felt you couldn't."

It's not terrible to forget that, there are lots of things I can't remember. Part of doing this is to bring all those individual memories together. Annie[6] spoke. My father read a passage from *The Prophet*[7] by Khalil Gibran. Cathy read a poem[8] – she was the only one of the children who did. It wasn't particularly a poem about Abi, not one she liked, just one Cathy chose.

Do you remember much about how the children were? How I was?

"I remember more about how you were and I felt very, very close to you. Sort of that we were pulled together. I can't remember how soon it was, but I had the feeling that if we were away from our house we were going to meet people and we would just deal with that; if they couldn't deal with it, that was their problem. I suspect I didn't want to be away from you."

---

[6] Paddy's next eldest sister.
[7] See appendix p.229.
[8] See appendix p.229.

Because you wanted to be with me or were worried about me?

"I wasn't worried you'd do something stupid. No, I wanted to protect you. You were pretty – I can't find the word here... putting armour on. Sullen doesn't convey what I mean properly."

Not my usual perky self then!

"Less than that! But that was OK, I had the same feeling about you that I did about me: however you felt or behaved was OK because the worst thing in the world had happened to us."

Did you ever wonder if we would manage to stay together?

"No, I felt that we had been through it differently four years earlier when the baby died. Even though the magnitude of it couldn't compare, I did feel we had got through a really difficult time once before. There were lots of practical things to deal with then, particularly since the children were younger and more dependent. This time I resolved that when I went back to work I was going to spend more time with you and the children. I was going to come home earlier and appreciate you more. I don't know if it felt like I did that to you?"

I'm not sure, I remember now you've reminded me of it. I suppose one difference for us was that you had your work and I didn't have that at all.

"Work was something I used to help me to deal with it. To work and to work well, actually I did some things much more efficiently. People didn't know how to talk to me

about it. I'd just go in and get on with my work without interruption, finish and come home."

Who do you think helped? If anybody did...

"You did. The kindness of colleagues helped; John Knox, for instance. The next year I went away to a conference in Dublin, I had been supposed to go to a conference the week after Abi died, so to leave you and go away six months later for a few days was a big challenge. I didn't want to go and be with people I didn't know. I don't know what persuaded me to go, whether it was you or someone else, but it was a fairly late decision. People were very kind and supportive, without necessarily referring to Abi. One woman in particular just took me in hand. It was so hard meeting new people and them asking me that dreadful question – how many children have you got? Do you have children?

Also people at work helped. I don't know how conscious I was of it, but as soon as I started reflecting, I realised the pain it had caused people – because it could have been them. I think people did care about me, because I was hurting so much it hurt them. I don't remember talking to my secretary, Mary, or the nurses on my wards, but they were always very supportive and protective.

Our children just being there helped. There was nothing they particularly did or said. They were going through it too. I felt like I loved them even more because of Abi dying. It was as if they were even more precious than they had been before?

All those letters which came – did I reply to them all? I suppose those letters brought it home to me that it did matter to other people. A lot of them didn't know Abi; it was me or us that they knew. The more emotive ones were from people who did know her."

It was an affirmation that she mattered and we mattered.

You've had four major bereavements – how does losing Abi compare to losing your parents?

"When my mother died, it was much easier for me because she was 81 and not in the best of health. She had accepted she was going to die fairly soon. That doesn't mean it wasn't a shock though. Dad was only 58 and it was a much more difficult experience.

You've reminded me as we've been talking about Abi, about the anger I also felt when our baby died earlier on. I had a lot of anger about medical incompetence and the way you were treated. That was a much more private grief, though. As far as other people were concerned, you were pregnant and then it ended. Whereas for us you had had a little person inside you and we had had all our plans and our vision of what things were going to be like for months. They were personal to us.

With Abi it was much more public; so many people knew. One of my strong recollections was of the impact she made on people – maybe I was just a proud father, but I had the feeling that she had made more impact than you would expect of a two year old child, just by the force of her personality. I remember Annie commenting on it."

I must have talked to you about this next part – what was Abi for, why did we have her, her role, why was she alive for only three short years? I can't find an answer. When you grow to be an adult and live a full life, you can see your impact. For you, the number of people you have cared for and influenced makes that impact even more. This writing is part of her impact on our family. It's taken all this time, almost into the adulthood she never had, to come to fruition. For me it's making sense of it now.

"I think with some exceptions she has made us a stronger family. She was a focus that united us, like those evenings in that long sitting room at 126 when she was the centre of attention and we were all focussed on her. I think the fact of her having died gives a powerful connection between us all.

We realised that despite those strong connections and memories, we all had a sense of isolation within us.

"One of the things you talked about in the early stages was how you and I dealt with our grief at different stages. We shared things, but still there were times when one of us had a good day and the other a bad day. It was the same with the kids; Cathy was wrapped up in her grief when we felt she should be moving on. It's too strong to say we were cross with her but we got frustrated with her and didn't really understand it."

I remember you yelling at me once when we were sitting in our bedroom "Why can't you move on?" There was frustration in you too. You said maybe I needed to see a psychiatrist or something.

"I developed a coping mechanism that you didn't buy into and I found that quite frustrating. Mine was related to the fact that the only reason I was sad was because when she was alive she was such a good thing. Because of the extent of how good and lovely she was I don't need to be sad. And it worked. It was a strategy but it did work. I could smile about her."

Do you think those different ways of coping with Abi's death damaged our relationship at all?

"Not sure, I don't know what might have happened if she hadn't died. We've had our ups and downs."

One thing was that if Abi hadn't died, I might not have got into the work I do and what I have learned and experienced has been a real benefit to us.

"I have never doubted for a moment that I wanted to be with you, which I think I did before. I just questioned it; I never decided I didn't want to be with you when things weren't going well. What are we in this relationship for if it's not making us happy? But I hardly remember the issue arising in my mind except at my lowest of lows. I never thought, 'What's the point in trying to get through this, I may as well just walk away'."

Did you ever think I might?

"Yes, I think I did. My most powerful time when I thought you wanted to leave me was when you came back from your residential[9]. My imagination was running riot but I don't think that was directly connected to Abi. Though you had been doing work about Abi: you knew that but I didn't, you felt distant from me and very different. Once you had talked to me and I could understand what had happened, it was OK."

So you didn't just want to prove the statistics wrong (of

---

[9]   During the residential element of my training as a counsellor, I had had a major breakthrough in understanding how come I had found the years since Abi died so difficult. I wanted to share what had happened with Paddy but the house was full when I returned home and I wanted it to be private between the two of us.

couples breaking up), even though that would be in your character.

"It was different – I knew it was a risk therefore I was forewarned if ever there was anything happening that threatened our relationship, I wanted to deal with it."

Suppose that might have been counter-productive at times.

"Yes, definitely it was."

You wanted to rush in, whereas I needed some space...

"I think I believed in you more than you did. When you were going back to work and applying for jobs – I was convinced you could do anything."

That job I applied for as a transplant co-ordinator! That wouldn't have been the right job for me at all. I am doing now what I want to be doing and am good at doing. I knew I needed to find some work to do, but before that I thought having another child would be what would really help.

There was yet another hurdle because of your vasectomy when Abi was about nine months old, so we knew you would have to have a reversal before anything else. I had never had any problems getting pregnant before, so I assumed that would still be the case. What are your thoughts now about the invasive techniques we underwent?

"I'm angry with myself for having had a vasectomy in the first place. It was a hasty decision and I don't know what it was based on. I think I normally consider all the angles

carefully, and that decision was based on protecting you from more hurt after the stillbirth, the Caesarean section and the miscarriage. With hindsight it was a stupid thing to have done. I'm not sure it was a sensible decision that we didn't want any more children at that stage. It wasn't even financial logic about not affording more children."

It wouldn't have been the end of the world if I had got pregnant again.

"As we discovered years later... It was cold logic rather than sense. Then when I had it reversed, it felt very, very important that it was successful and we would be able to have another baby. I don't really know how we decided we wanted another child."

It was quite soon after Abi died. I can remember clinging onto each other and me crying that all I wanted was another baby. As I look back, I think it would have been to take up my mind, stop me thinking about Abi, heal the pain that way. I know now that wasn't the way it was to work for me.

"I remember the feeling that no-one could replace her. Another child would be an interloper, would be a pale imitation, which is stupid because it would have been our child, but it felt like he or she would be like a fraud. Then we decided we did want another baby. I wanted to try and help to heal you."

So it was more for me than you?

"It would have been for me too, but I didn't desperately want another child. I thought the only way to mend your broken heart was to have another child. It would have given you something positive to deal with. We changed

GPs and talked to the new GP about it. I had the reversal and then you didn't get pregnant.

I felt steam-rollered into the GIFT[10] process. Suddenly we were into technology. The consultant we saw was expecting something. I don't know what. I needed to have sperm counts to see what was going on; it just seemed to take over. I suppose if it had worked, the world would have been a different place. We had three cycles, and I can remember coming to a very quick decision together that we didn't want to do that again. No doubt it was the right decision at the time. The whole thing was absolutely dreadful – it shattered all our hopes and it was just too much to bear."

Part of our secrecy about our hopes and plans was thinking that we'll tell people when we have this joyous news and they will be so excited and pleased for us. But it never happened.

Then I did get pregnant naturally and very unexpectedly in 1994, and we did tell people then. I suppose it was better that we had and that they knew about it because when I had the miscarriage they could help to support us.

"I think it was hard to accept, but easier in the great scheme of things. Compared with losing Abi, it was a disappointment; painful. I remember the joy of it, of seeing the blue line in the pregnancy kit – your disbelief at it. What was amazing was the instant joy; the realisation that the joy was there all the time, that we were ready for it. And then having it whipped away. I don't remember

---

[10] GIFT is another description of IVF technology. It requires considerable medical intervention: drugs to stimulate the ovaries; procedures to extract the eggs and mix with sperm in the hope of fertilisation; followed by implantation back into the uterus.

the pain being in the same league. It was just not the same
– didn't come close to, not even to the experience of losing
the other baby."

I suppose it was shocking because we never expected
me to get pregnant again after the GIFT experiences. My
mother said I might have got pregnant very easily, but
every time I was pregnant there were problems.

We ended our conversation here.

I know it was a truly valuable time, stimulating many
thoughts and memories for both of us. What follows are
my reflections, understandings and insights[11] as a result
of our conversation.

When Paddy talked about Abi's time in hospital, he was
really upset, and the memory of that time is very vivid
for me too. I remember how quiet it seemed to be, that I
knew what would be coming when Paddy and the surgeon
walked through the door. It was like waiting for the axe
to fall. I can't remember whether I had said anything to
prepare our parents, or if Paddy had. I don't know if they
knew what was going to happen, if they were prepared in
any way. I thought the surgeon's words were so bald, so
brutal. I hated him at that moment. There was no room
for compromise. **This was it.**

One thing Paddy couldn't remember was whether she had
a tube in her mouth or a tracheotomy. My recollection is
that it was a tracheotomy – because I can recall her little
mouth and kissing her lips at the time. And that is a
different reminder of just how important her mouth was.
She was so articulate for a little child; she had humour;

---

[11] This process of recording the interview followed by my own reflections is
the pattern for each person's chapter.

60

she understood how to be amusing; how to make jokes; she loved kissing people; she loved eating and relished her food.

One thing we both remembered strongly though – and which I imagine is in the children's thoughts too – were the evenings we spent together. It was the time after supper when it was too early to begin the bath and bedtime rituals – my memory is that it was often springtime and it being just that bit too cold to go outside in the garden to play. The children would play games, made-up ones, in our sitting room and it's true that Abi was the centre of attention. The other three were enjoying the time with her when they had been away at school during the day; they taught her tricks and songs and so on.

I thought about the way Paddy tortured himself after Abi had died, thinking that if she had been at home when she had stopped breathing he could have saved her by doing a tracheotomy. Would he really have been able to do that? I know I always found it very hard when he talked about it, because I immediately began to imagine what might have happened, what he might have done, what it would have been like. And if he had, and she had still died, how could we have lived with that?

When Paddy talked about Elspeth leaving Abi to go another hospital, I heard myself trying to make it OK; I heard myself trying to excuse Elspeth and perhaps Paddy too. This was because I knew he felt guilty about what happened for a long time afterwards. Perhaps I was doing that because it is easier to do that than face the fact I am angry with her too. And I was, for a long time afterwards.

My memory of the meeting with Elspeth is that I felt very uncomfortable about him being angry. I don't think I had ever heard him talk like that and be so angry before. I got an inkling of how Paddy was at work, how steadfast in his views, how strong in his opinions. He was scary and I felt frightened. Another part of me envied him being able to be that articulate and put into words what he felt. I just wasn't able to do that at that point. I think perhaps that meeting was very important for Paddy in the whole process of accepting what had happened and expressing his feelings. He had had that outlet; my way of accepting what had happened was much slower and it was a long time before I could let myself express my anger.

The subtext behind all these thoughts was almost impossible to acknowledge in my heart and mind. The situation we experienced of a lack of medical staff on hand and the fact that there was a seriously ill baby across the city actually didn't matter. If that baby had died because doctors were saving our daughter, we wouldn't have known anything about it and Abi would still be alive. It's that terrible choice – who do we save? We didn't know at the time what was going to happen.

I felt I now knew even more about how it had been for Paddy. In the early years after she died, we talked a lot about Abi, the whys, what it meant, what we could do, how were we coping. Naturally those conversations petered out over the years though, from time to time, we would talk again about her. We might have heard or read something about a similar situation. As I developed my work as a counsellor and mentor[12], I began to learn and understand about how people make sense of the difficulties and traumas they have in their lives. I realised

---

[12] I work from a developmental, whole person learning perspective, with experience in working with the transpersonal dimension, therapeutic massage as well as 'talking' therapies.

that for my own sanity, I needed to find a way to keep Abi where she could help me. It did me no good at all to agonise over the experience.

The experience of our talking again about the intensity of Abi's illness and death highlighted aspects I had never really considered before. I realised more strongly what a different experience it was for both of us. In a way, I was very protected in the bubble of just being with her in the hospital. Paddy had all the coming and going, having to relate to people and telling people. Some people would make crass comments and that must have been really hard to deal with. And, of course, they were only crass because people didn't realise the magnitude of the situation.

Paddy had to get in touch with his work, he had to phone our parents and tell them. I don't think this even occurred to me at the time. This made me realise that Paddy had done all of that. I had done nothing; I can't even remember if I thought I should be doing it, or if I wasn't able to do it, or what. It emphasises just how much he looked after me, and did what needed doing. I was oblivious to so much. I find this quite shocking as I think I've always been the one in our relationship who considers the wider picture of what needs doing. I see myself as being the one who plans and manages things – but not in this situation. I see how I lost myself completely. I feel I was swallowed up by what was happening in front of me on a second by second basis. The outside world wasn't important at all, to such an extent that I don't think I even worried about the other children much. I was totally focussed on my daughter and what was happening to her.

I also realised in a new way one of the huge difficulties of being a doctor who has a child who is ill and maybe dying.

Paddy has a huge loyalty towards the NHS and a deep understanding of the problems for doctors with under-staffed units who have to cover more than one hospital and make decisions about which child to treat, where to devote time, energy and expertise. He had already faced the dilemma of being a relative and a doctor when his father died of leukaemia when aged just 58, and again when our unborn baby died. The difficulty then was that I was ill with a badly fractured arm and therefore under the care of the orthopaedic team whilst also being 36 weeks pregnant. The obstetric team should have been consulted as to the best treatment for my baby, they weren't and our baby died two days after my accident. Although I was told that there was no connection between the accident and the baby dying, inevitably I felt it was my fault.

As a 'medical parent', possessing knowledge and coming up against what could be seen as incompetence, or negligence, what do you do? Which side do you come down on? Inevitably the parent must win out, and then you may end up with feelings of impotence, having put yourself in the hands of other professionals. You then have to deal with the consequences of the whole catastrophic mess.

Then there was the challenging situation Paddy was in of having to return to work in the same building and with the possibility of seeing the same staff around the hospital. He had to face the prospect of caring for his patients on ICU and working with relatives who were facing bereavements themselves. All these factors were facing Paddy as the situation unfolded and he had to deal with these difficulties, and many more, over the years that we spent in Hull after Abi died.

Paddy insisted on being present during the medical discussions about the viability of Abi's life. I realised how important that was to him, and I can imagine that it would be to me too in other circumstances. This experience has taught me a lot about what I want when my parents die, or if Paddy dies before me. I want to be involved and I want to be there. And I want the support from others to encourage me to be there, even if I am upset. It will help me in the long run to get through the situation, to remember with clarity rather than fantasising about what was done, or not, in the event of a medical emergency.

Paddy and I have talked at much length about the kind of parents we wanted to be. The experience of Abi's death brought that home to us in an even more acute way. We discussed over and over again what we did then, how we could perhaps have done it differently. How we could have been better parents. We try so hard as parents to protect our children, but there comes a point when we have to leave our children alone. They have to become adults. There are many situations in life when something doesn't quite work out and you go back and try again, maybe by doing things differently. This was the ultimate situation when we couldn't do that.

As a parent you practise on the first child and hope it gets a little bit easier with each one you have. We kept trying to be better parents.

I think this was the point at which I became an adult and left the fairy-tale of childhood behind. Life wasn't going to be how I had planned it. I think about it now and realise I was 34, the age Cathy is now. I thought I was an adult then, and that I knew how to cope with life. For the most part I did, having a big family to care for meant that I was pretty self-reliant and I thought I knew what I was doing most of the time. But this - this was another experience altogether. I felt very alone in it, I wanted to be helped, to be looked after, but I didn't know how to ask for help. I didn't really know what I wanted. We tried to carry on without asking for help, to be independent.

Elspeth suggested we talk to a social worker with particular experience and expertise in helping families who had lost a child. I think this must have been pretty soon after Abi died. Paddy and I had an absolute conviction we would stay together, no matter how hard it was sometimes, and I felt this was not just about us and our relationship; it was also about the children and not wanting to put them through anything else that was traumatic.

As I talked to the family I became aware that our mothers and my father were trying to protect Paddy and me, just as we were attempting to protect all our children. All the mothers and all the fathers were trying to protect their children. But there comes a point when you just cannot do that. It doesn't matter whether your child is three or 33, they have to experience life on their own.

Our conversation also reminded me how envious I sometimes felt of Paddy being able to walk out of the house and into another environment that wasn't full of reminders; although, of course, there were lots of memories for him in the hospital. Many times I felt trapped at home. I know I was extremely lucky in being surrounded by many friends who were very caring and visited me most days, but sometimes I was just so tired of company and having to make an effort. I suspect I thought I 'should' be coping better than I was, that I should be 'getting over it'. And I think I probably gave the impression I was coping better than I really was. I did feel guilty about getting so tired of people coming round, knowing that it must have been hard for people to make the time for me. If only I had had the courage to say what I needed rather than avoiding it!

Paddy's reference to our first baby who had died and the way I was treated reminded me of that time. Because of my accident and injury before she died, there had to be an investigation. I assume this means the baby had a post-mortem and as far as I know her cause of death was unexplained. But the forensic pathologist had to inform the police, and the police had to come to interview me at home to ascertain the cause of the fall I had.

They asked me, bluntly, whether my husband had pushed me. I hadn't expected this: I was lying in bed, having given birth to a stillborn child the day before, bleeding, in a lot of pain from a fractured arm. It was the unthinkable, so ridiculous I couldn't really believe what they were asking me. I understand now that they were doing their job, but at the time it seemed the final straw.

And of course I also had to tell Paddy, and my mother, what they had asked me. Much of the feelings I had at that time became buried. Our other children were quite young and life was pretty difficult. Our way of coping with the loss was for me to become pregnant again as soon as I could. There came a point after Abi died when I realised I needed to grieve for that other daughter too, who had never even been given a proper name by us.

Abi had a strong personality and there were experiences we had of feeling her with us, as if she was sitting right there between us. One was within the first year quite near to home; another very strong experience was a long time afterwards when we were on holiday in France. We had had a wonderful holiday and really enjoyed the sunshine and the lazy days. We were on our way home when all of a sudden I could see Abi in the car standing between us. She had her hand on both our shoulders and was looking between us with a lovely smile on her face. It was as if she was saying, you two are OK, you've made it this far, you can be happy again without me. It was such a great, warm, peaceful feeling that washed over me. The wonderful thing about Paddy was that when I told him I could see her, he just asked me what she looked like, what she was wearing. He had no trace of envy in his voice. He is a wonderful man.

Five

Matthew

Matthew is now a confident young man, forging a successful career for himself as a Director within Health Service Management. He has always been larger than life, in every sense of the word. When he was a small child, being tall for his age, strangers would frequently talk to him and expect an answer which was way beyond his understanding or linguistic capabilities.

I had wanted to have children for a long time and so when he was born I threw myself into motherhood, and, despite it being quite a lonely time for me with few friends around, I loved being a Mum. He and I had a very close relationship for his first months, but things did change once Cathy was born – she was a difficult baby and needed a lot of my time and attention, and I think Matthew lost out.

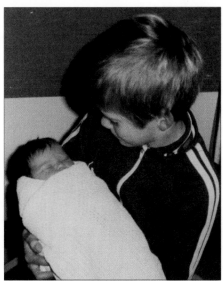

Matthew holding Abi
the evening after she was born

He was a sociable child and by then we were living in a place that was teeming with children; they were always in and out of one another's houses. Matthew learnt

*Matthew's expression conveys
his pride and love for Abi*

rapidly to get attention by being naughty. He was adorable looking, with blond hair and an angelic smile, even when he had been a little devil.

He had responsibilities put upon him at a young age with his younger siblings arriving, but he appeared to enjoy it and loved having them to play with. As Cathy remarks later, he and Simon loved to play rough and tumble with Abi; she loved it too, despite the comparatively large age difference between them.

Matthew would invent games – like 'the panty gang' which involved all four children stripped down to their pants before bed-time and then charging up and down the room, racing from one end to another. He was excellent at whipping up excitement and energy; often the children had to be sent to run round the block to get rid of excess energy before bath-time. Usually Matthew was the ring-leader in this.

On the day Abi was born, Matthew came to visit me along with Paddy whilst the other two children were put to bed. I think he held a lot of responsibility for Abi – and he was devastated when she died. He said that evening that he could never be happy again. Later on I found it was impossible to get him to talk about her. I tried to draw him out, but nothing seemed to work. Because the whole process was so distressing for him, and for me, essentially there came a time when I think I gave up.

Looking back I can see perhaps this was the wrong thing to do, that we should have found another person for him to talk to and maybe that would have made a difference to him as he grew up. But again, we decided we knew best and were guided by having faith in ourselves and feeling we instinctively knew the best approach. He would be in tears if I attempted to bring Abi into the conversation; he became withdrawn and this was when he was 11 years old and growing rapidly.

He was involved with everything at school – sport, music and was extremely bright; he never had to work particularly hard to get good results. He directed his grief into being naughty again – he would play up in lessons and if he came across a 'weak' teacher he knew instantly how to exploit that. He made the class laugh; he disrupted lessons; he was sent out of the class. Parents' evenings grew to be something Paddy and I often dreaded; teacher after teacher would complain about his behaviour, whilst at the same time acknowledging that he could produce excellent results very easily. It was only the odd one or two teachers who knew how to handle him and earned his respect. He was rebelling in his own way and perhaps this was his way of forgetting about Abi's death and his grief – or putting it away in a box.

Before we began to talk I checked that he was happy enough to carry on with our discussion. This felt important because when I first mentioned it he had sounded ambivalent and unsure what help he could be.

I started by saying that my purpose was not to just make people upset but for it to be helpful, and so far it had been.

I want very much to find a way to liberate us, so it's more possible to talk more freely without getting upset. I am also hoping that some memories will return and that some of the gaps can be filled for all of us. I had a great experience talking to my mother; she had so many vivid memories. We had a really good time, we cried and we laughed and it was lovely.

"I agree with your hopes and think it might be helpful for us all. I realise that we seldom talk about Abi when we are all together, and that is a pity. We haven't shared as much as perhaps we could and so in that sense I don't think we've helped one another as much as we could have.

Your ideas make sense to me. I didn't think the purpose was just to ask questions and get me upset. I think it's a really good idea, and something for us to look at will be helpful. But I'm worried I can't remember much."

What memories do you have of the time when she died? Would you like me to fill in any gaps you might have?

"It's all very difficult to recall, because it's upsetting. I've suppressed my memories."

(Matthew became very distressed at this point, caused, he said, by the pain of the memories.)

"I remember her being in hospital and going to visit her. There were things you told us after that but I don't remember for myself. I remember when we were told that she had died. The doctor came to us, but I can't remember what his exact words were."

Was that the first time you knew she would die?

"I'm not sure. I don't know whether I sort of knew and I suppressed it. Afterwards, I guess it was later on, I remember saying to you, and this is a clear memory, I wished it had been me rather than her. I remember thinking about that quite a lot, and you told me not to be stupid. Well, not that exactly but that thought."

Do you have a memory of her in hospital?

"Yes, I remember standing next to her cot, being with her."

(It was hard for him to get the words out at this point.)

Any memories of your feelings round that time? You were 11; do you think you knew what was happening?

"You said I had asked you if she was going to die, and you said she wouldn't – you said how awful you felt about saying that. I don't remember that though."

You were peeling potatoes for supper the night Abi went into hospital; a very vivid memory for me.

"I don't remember that."

I stayed in hospital with Abi, Granny came to help us, Dad went back and forth between home and the hospital. You, Cathy and Simon went to school the first day, but then had some time off school.

Do you have any questions you wanted to ask at the time but didn't? Why it happened, or any other questions like that?

"I never felt that I wanted to know more; I asked you about it just four or five years ago, how she died and so on. When I was little I don't think I knew how she died. I knew it was to do with her breathing, but I didn't think about why, what had caused it or anything like that. The only thing was how unfair it seemed; the only thing I wanted was to be able to travel through time and change it. I don't think I really felt a need to understand more. I just wanted it not to be."

What kind of effect do you think Abi's dying had on you?

"I think it made me less concerned about the consequences of my actions. It made me feel that it doesn't matter what goes wrong in my life, nothing could be worse than that – although it isn't helpful to make comparisons. I began to have some ideas which took shape about a year or so ago and I've a theory that it made me unable to make lasting relationships with girls because I had a place in my heart reserved for her. All of my feelings and emotions about her were held on the inside; I don't share them with anyone else."

(He was able to laugh about this at this point and was a bit frustrated with the difficulty of describing what he meant.)

"I can't put them into words. I thought maybe the love of my life was Abi, and while I'm holding all these feelings inside me for her, I wouldn't be able to give myself properly to someone else. I straight away realised it wasn't a good thing and resolved to try to talk to friends much more and mention her, and try to bring her to my surface instead of having her buried deep inside me. I actively put the effort in and mentioned her to people, then I stopped doing it."

What was it like talking about her more, was it as hard as you thought?

"No, it was probably easier than I thought it would be."

I've a very clear memory of being in the Lake District one holiday – I guess you might have been 12 or 13. We were walking along a country lane and I was trying so hard to make you talk about Abi, but you just wouldn't, I decided then not to push you. I just thought I couldn't do it anymore. Partly I imagine it was too painful for me too. But when I look back I feel like I let you down then, I should have found some way of helping you more. It sounds like you made a conscious decision then to bury it – a very quick decision.

When you were a teenager, I sometimes wondered how much you thought about Abi, just because you didn't talk about her, or very rarely. I know that can't be true. Deep down you had those very strong feelings and emotions, and also lots of your friends knew Abi. What was it like for you, going back to school?

"One thing I remember from school was about a friend who had come to stay with us a few months before Abi died."

I remember. He had really taken to Abi and played with her a lot – including giving her sweets to eat before supper time, which was against our 'house rules' and infuriated me!

"He and I had drifted apart later but a few months after she died he came up to me and he asked me about Abi and how she was. His first question was about her, not about the others. I just looked at him and said, 'Well, she's dead'. He thought I was messing around as kids do – and I wouldn't talk about it. He said, 'no she's not, you're joking'. Another friend told him that she was dead and to shut up and go away.

Another thing about burying everything is that I keep my feelings about Abi very private – I don't know why because it's the same for you and all of us. It's not like she was mine and not yours. I think I've not wanted to talk about her because she's sacred and I don't want to share my feelings with other people. Friends at school knew her, but until I was in my late 20s there were only a handful of people I'd ever told about her and what happened."

What changed in your late 20s?

"My girlfriend at the time said she thought it was a shame that I hid her away, I should be proud of her. She bought me a little photo frame – to have a picture of her around. Before that I remember going for a curry in London with friends when I hadn't long been living there. I had a photo of an ex-girlfriend and a photo of Abi in my wallet. I was paying the bill, got my wallet out and left it on the table while I went to the toilet. The others had gone through it

and left the photos on the table. They all started laughing and asking about them. I was so angry with them; I threw some money on the table and went home. I went back to my room and cried and cried. Kev, who's a very close friend, came up and asked me what was wrong. I wanted to tell him about Abi, but just couldn't."

What stopped you?

"That feeling that I don't want to burden others with my loss. When I think about it, I can rationalise it and think, well it's not their loss. If a friend of mine told me a similar story, it wouldn't hit me in the way that I worry my story might be hitting them. I think they would feel mortified but maybe I think it's a bigger deal for other people than it really is."

Often what happens is they don't know what to say, so you are the one who has to manage the situation and you're the person who's had the loss, feels vulnerable and upset.

"I hate that. It just puts me off talking about her – I can't be jolly about it and say don't worry about it and I'm fine when that isn't how I feel.

I worry that my memory of her is only loss and sorrow and regret, not about what a nice person she is. I can't remember very much about what we did together."

Does it help when we are all together and we start talking to bring memories back? What she was like when she was alive?

"Yes, but I still find it difficult whenever she is mentioned – I start crying. Sometimes I feel I wallow in self-pity and

that my sorrow is just about me, it's nothing to do with Abi. I'm upset and want to have something to cry about. I worry, but don't know that it's right."

I might be wrong, but do you think you use the fact of her death as an excuse or a reason for the ways in which you behave or approach things?

"I don't think I do consciously – sometimes it's an excuse for feeling sad. What I've done over the years is to just have some time when I'm on my own in my bedroom. I go and be quiet and spend some time thinking about her and getting really upset, getting the emotions out of my system. It's become less frequent over time; it used to be every day, now it's less and less. I describe it as burying my feelings, but I found a way to let them out."

You've described having some quiet time and letting your feelings come up, that isn't burying it.

"My feelings are always sorrow, anger, regret."

Anger with?

"The world. It's quite a long time since I've had that quiet time to remember her actually. I've moved the picture I carry round of her in my wallet, so every time I open my wallet I see her. The photo doesn't look that dated, so you wouldn't know it was taken so long ago. It's an easy way for people to ask me about who it is, so it helps. Sometimes I say it's me and my little sister who died. Sometimes it brings questions from others, but not often. Checkout people in Sainsbury's ask me sometimes! I'm glad I have done that, it means my feelings have come out more. It's helped me."

One of the things for me was that it wasn't just my loss. For me it was also about being a wife and mother to you three children who are grieving: how can I help you all as well as me? We each have had that – our particular role and place in the family. I've wondered about the way in which losing Abi affected you as children: for you as the eldest, Simon's youngest role and the changing nature of that, and Cathy's loss of her only sister. Ever since you were a little boy, people have taken you for being older and more responsible than you were – I remember even when you were a one year old in the butcher's, people would talk to you and expect you to reply, when you were far too young to understand what they were saying. I wondered if you had any feelings of too much being expected of you, and that was too much for you?

"It makes me think about the responsibility you and Dad gave us as children. I don't think I felt responsible for how Simon and Cathy were. I don't remember thinking I must make sure they are OK. I think I took the whole thing quite personally. That sounds selfish, but I didn't think about them. I don't think pressure was put on me to make sure they were OK. It never entered my head that perhaps I should have looked after Cathy and Simon more."

Do you have any memories of the funeral at all?

"Yes, the crematorium; something about a rose bush? What happened to her ashes? The memorial meeting was on the Saturday – I can't remember much about that either."

We asked you if you would read something, and you said you couldn't. Do you have any thoughts about us having that celebration of her life? Do you think it was a good idea, or what about the timing – was it too soon?

"Yes, now I do think it was a good idea but I don't know what I thought at the time. I wonder whether my reaction might have been that I don't want to share this with other people. In retrospect, I think it's a good idea, and to have had it soon after she died."

What about when Granny died? You won't remember Grandpa.

"I've one memory of him – of sitting in the kitchen on his knee and him reading 'The Three Billy Goats Gruff' to me. Years before Granny Nel died I had thought about the fact that she might die. It was completely different, nothing like Abi dying. Granny had done loads of stuff in her life; she was happy and she died in a peaceful way. I can talk about Granny without crying; I don't feel I've buried anything about her. I feel that was a normal grieving process. I just think the process I went through when Abi died was absolutely not normal."

Any idea how you would like things to be? Would you like to talk about Abi more?

"I want it to be how it is. I've buried feelings about her and my loss and I think that has been what has worked for me. But I would like to be able to talk about her more easily."

I guess the way to do it is to keep on doing it, because it gets easier the more you do it. Maybe the more we are able to talk about Abi to people who didn't know her at all and maybe if we can be more matter-of-fact that might help a little. If the only people we talk to about her are close members of the family, what happens is that we trigger off emotion in one another and it makes it harder to talk in a more down to earth manner.

"I like the way she has a very special place in my heart, so when I do talk about her to someone, it really means something."

Was there anyone who helped?

"The only people I've ever talked to in any depth have been my family and my girlfriends. All of them have helped in some way. With girlfriends, I've chosen a time to tell them and we've spent time talking about her. I've spent more time talking with them than with any of the family. Because I've had quite a lot of girlfriends it's got easier with time, so really the whole thing has got easier with time. I used to spend time every day alone, thinking about her and crying, but gradually that has got less and less – it has probably been about a year since I've done that.

Dad has said to me how you always feel low mid-November to mid-December; I don't have that, I like to remember her birthday and the day she died – though her birthday is more important. I think about her then and spend some time on my own. I used to never go out on her birthday and I would spend time at home on my own, not doing fun things. It was more just to think about her."

Have you ever thought about, or wished we did something as a family to mark her birthday?

"No, it hadn't occurred to me. It would be difficult and painful for me. Sometimes I drive in my car and think that the thing I want most in the world is to talk to her. I wish I had just picked her up from the train station or the airport. I find it hard to imagine what she would be like – I imagine Cathy and the Abi I remember, a kind of amalgamation of the two of them, yet her personality was nothing like Cathy's. I just can't remember very much about her."

In lots of ways she was quite shy and clingy, yet in other ways she was very confident.

"Cathy is very shy when she doesn't know people – even though she's grown-up she can still be like that."

One of the things people commented on after she died was about her strong personality, and one question I have had was about her purpose, what she was here for. I have never found the answer, have you thought about it?

"Without getting into the why and exploring religious beliefs, I don't think there is an answer. It just happened and there isn't a reason, the fact that she died and she was young – that's it. It was horrible, but no more than that."

Church – Dad and I never believed in a God, but perhaps you did and her dying maybe changed that?

"Ever since I was a young child I hadn't believed in a God – I remember talking about this with a friend when I was about seven. I don't know where I got the idea from, not you and Dad – you didn't talk about it. I developed that idea somehow. My views haven't changed!"

You've said you hold a special place in your heart for Abi – have you ever felt her with you?

"No, I wish I had. Don't know what the difference is between that and thinking about her. I feel like I'm opening up a mind that is very blank."

Some people have very clear memories which are like a series of snapshots rather than a memory of an event which might be more like a film running in their head. You've talked about your feelings a lot. This process is partly about me wanting to pull together a picture of what happened, but it is more about how we have coped.

How we have coped isn't wrong – it's what it has been like. It's such an isolating experience – even in a marriage, because it is different for each person. Different aspects have different meanings and impact for men and women, and each man and each woman.

Photos are fine but it's the family conversations about things we did that really bring back the memories.

My mother remembered Abi in Dundee, and she must have been quite young – Si had been naughty and threatened with being sent out. Abi sat in her high-chair and pointed at him saying loudly, "You – out." How funny she was, even though she was quite little, she could get the joke and make a joke too.

Sometimes we'd go and pick up Cathy and Simon from school, all go swimming and then drop Cathy off at Brownies afterwards on our way home. Looking back it was a logistical nightmare. You children had tea at Haltemprice pool – sausage and chips – what a treat!! But it was all we could afford, and I don't even know how often we did it. It seems like many times but it probably wasn't really. Being able to do it depended on all four of you not being ill, having a cold or something.

"I remember a Leadership course I was doing a while ago. In the first coaching session, the coach said, 'Tell me about when you were little'. I told her about Abi – it all came pouring out. She said in a later session that we hadn't come back to talk about that again, and she clearly was

seeing if I would open up a bit more. I didn't take that opportunity though."

Have you ever thought about having children of your own? Do you want children? Are you frightened about what could happen and whether you could cope?

"Yes, and I don't want to blindly assume I can have as many children as I can – I had an idea I would have four. Now I've started thinking about whether to have children at all. I've always thought if I did have children and they were ill, how would I handle it? Would I just rush them to hospital? I might be a nightmare as a father or a husband."

Surely more important than having children is being with the right person?

"The chances of finding someone you want to be with are difficult – some people think you shouldn't have children because it isn't the kind of world you want to bring people into. I've been thinking about that, but I'm not sure that I agree with it. If you weren't able to have children, that could help you come to terms with it. At least they aren't in a world where they could be raped, hurt or die young."

That would be understandable. Perhaps things just work out in the way they work out. You meet the person and if you make that decision to talk about Abi more and get your feelings out more, it will enable you to let them in and yourself out. So perhaps the decision whether to have children or not will resolve itself according to the person you meet, whether you do decide to spend your lives together, whether or not you decide to have children and whether you can have them together.

"Not telling people I have known for 13 or 14 years gets more difficult with more time elapsing, I don't want to do it when I've had a bit to drink either."

Do you have any thoughts or feelings about when I got pregnant later on?

"At the time I was really worried that you were pregnant to take the place of Abi. I put that to one side, and I just thought no, this is different. It was nice and exciting, when you told us in the dining room at 112. You said we've got some news and I said, 'You're pregnant!' You asked how I knew that. I thought that if you are breaking some news to us this formally, you're either getting divorced or you're pregnant. And I don't think you're getting divorced! I told some people at University as well, I got a postcard later on in the year from someone, something about you'll have a little brother or sister now."

We wound up our conversation at this point; it had clearly been emotional for us both, but I thought it was helpful and to some extent had filled in some gaps for Matthew. As well as that, some of the issues I had worried about over the years and blamed myself for were laid to rest.

Talking to Matthew was the hardest conversation – I was unprepared for the depth of his feelings. Whilst I'd always known that he was upset and found it really hard to talk to me, and other people, about her, I thought he would be more reticent about his feelings or that they might have diminished over time. Instead of that, as soon as I asked him a question he became very emotional. He was hurting so much that he clutched his head and pulled his hair. It was very hard to be beside him and continue with what I had set out to do. It felt like real anguish; as if all of this was just below the surface, waiting to be released.

He later described that his thoughts and memories of that week of her being in hospital went round his head like a film.

It was hard for him to get the words out when he described standing next to Abi's cot in the hospital. I remembered my mother saying how it had been one of the most painful experiences of her life, watching him holding her hand and the tears just pouring onto Abi's arm.

I wondered if that was because his memories were of her death and the loss and sadness, rather than the happiness of her life and what she brought us. It felt as if he has blotted much of that out, he said more than once how much he wished he could remember more about her, what she was like.

I learned that though I have some vivid memories, like him peeling the potatoes, they were not at all strong for him. So I had worried about this for all those years, and yet it wasn't important for him at all... or at least it wasn't in his memory. I also realised that I didn't know for sure about his belief system – I thought I knew he didn't have any religious beliefs, but it was a guess. I wondered if he had believed and the fact of Abi's death had destroyed that. Matthew had been a Cub and then a Scout, so in fact had attended church from time to time, but we never attended church as a family.

He had blanked out a lot, I think, and I hope that when he comes to read this, and reads more of other people's memories of her and the time she was part of our lives, that it will help. He has obviously thought a lot about it over the years and worked out what he could do on his own and what helped him. I spent a lot of time when Matthew was younger wishing I could have been of more help. Through the process of the interviews and then writing this book, I have found that it has helped all three of my children to be able to talk more easily about Abi and it has also filled in some of the gaps in their memories.

During our conversation, we spent some time looking through a small album of photos of Abi and the family – because there was no access to video or digital photos then, it means we haven't got that much to draw on to access memories. He remembered a picture Cathy drew (she was about six at the time) of what Abi would be like when she was the same age. She drew Abi with dark hair which she had when she was born, which later changed to being very blonde.

We also talked about what it must have been like for the grandparents having an invasion of four lively children into their ordered existence when we went to stay. One photo showed my father sitting reading the newspaper in the background while mayhem was going on around him – I guess this was his way of retreating for a while. In lots of the photos Matthew is holding Abi because he was the eldest – entrusted with that responsibility. He talked about how he remembered trying to get her to stroke her eczema rather than scratch it, so that she did not raise weals or bleed.

We remembered the time when we had just moved to Hull and we hadn't managed to get him into the school we wanted because he had to wait for a school place. Matthew and Abi would play a lot together whilst the others were in school – my memory is that he used to have so much energy, which I tried to find ways to get him to use up. Often this was about sending him to the shops for me, then him getting back home on his bike and me 'remembering' just one more thing I had forgotten before. I think his energy then was endless – I could never seem to tire him out!

We talked about some of the camping holidays we had. We had a big tent with three bedrooms and kept trying the children in different pairs to see what worked best. On our first camping holiday, in Norfolk, we gave Matthew the responsibility to get Abi to sleep. It was so new and exciting in the tent, but she was really tired and battling to stay awake rather than give in and go off to sleep. Matthew and Paddy went in the Beetle while the rest of us drove down in the other car – two cars was the only way we could get all the gear there! The two of them ate peaches and the stones stayed in the front of the car for months afterwards as a reminder of the journey.

I don't want to feel full of regret and punish myself for things I think I should have done then, ways in which I might have been able to help the children more. I have more skills to help now, but that's because of the passage of time and because I've worked through my own process about this. In the first few years it was all so overwhelming. I wasn't able to do more to help Matthew – I could only do what I did at the time, and I did what I did with the best of intentions. I remember some occasions when I did try to shock him into talking about her – and I made him upset – and I feel bad about that now. I don't think it helped.

I remember a time when he was refusing to wear a reflective jacket, or even a reflective strap, across himself when he was cycling to school: it wasn't the 'cool' thing to do. The only way I seemed able to get through to him about how I felt was to scream, "I don't want to have another child of mine die!" It felt awful to do at the time, and feels awful now. It did shock him into being upset again, but I got through to him because he did wear something reflective. It had the effect and I got the outcome I wanted, but it was a horrible thing for me to put him through and feels very manipulative.

Whilst I imagine Matthew will always be upset to some extent when he thinks or talks about Abi, he is much more able to talk now. He has remembered more that we all shared together and he and I have been able to talk about events like the one I described above. Both of us remember it vividly and he confirmed for me that he did think I was being very manipulative, but he also told me not to give myself a hard time about it. I guess as parents we may all fall into that trap of finding underhand ways to get our children to do what we want them to do, rather than what they want to do – but that time did feel particularly horrible for me.

I feel that we've all managed to get here in spite of everything, not because of it. That we've done pretty well considering. I wish it could have been different, but it is as it's been and we have all had to live with it.

A few weeks after our conversation Paddy and I met Matthew when we were down for a weekend in London. We were walking through Regent's Park in brilliant sunshine on a freezing cold day. The park was full of joggers, skateboarders and people generally enjoying themselves in the sunshine. He told us that since he and I had talked he had remembered that when he began work in Hull at the hospital he was taken for an introductory tour around the wards and so on. He was taken into the Paediatric Intensive Care Unit and suddenly things began to appear awfully familiar: the layout of the room, the equipment he was seeing. All those buried memories for so long (11 years or so) began to shake themselves loose and rise up into his consciousness – like wreckage from a ship which has been lying on the bottom of the ocean for many years.

He had to try and communicate with the person showing him round in an intelligible and intelligent way, but at the same time he was trying to bury those memories and feelings again. It sounded as if he managed to do it, and then managed to block it out again. The power of our minds to push down unhappy and traumatic memories amazes me, but it seems like some of us have the ability, or need, to do that more than others. Matthew certainly has! It also struck me that although he was living at home with us at the time, he never mentioned that experience to us. It would have been an opening to talk about Abi a bit more, but he didn't take it up.

As we were walking round, he also said that he had been able to bring Abi into a conversation he had had the previous evening. His friends had been talking about significant dates, one of which happened to be her birthday. He found it natural enough to mention Abi, though the conversation didn't go into any kind of depth or touch any emotions. It felt like the beginning of a new chapter for Matthew though.

Matthew later told me how he thought about this concept of travelling through time and having the ability to change the outcome a lot. He used to spend quite a bit of time alone, thinking about Abi and crying about what had happened. This was something I hadn't known about.

Another aspect was that Matthew reads through the collection of cards and letters that people wrote to us after Abi died. He does this every couple of years. They include letters from his school and a note about the collection that the boys in his class raised on her behalf.

I wonder now whether, if I had known about both these things, it would have helped me because I would have realised that he was grieving in his own way. I spent a lot of time worrying that he was burying his feelings about her, but in fact that wasn't the case.

I feel these are both examples of having faith in the process of what needs to happen, and holding on to the idea that we all knew what we needed to do in our own way.

Matthew had quite a number of romantic relationships with some lovely young women through his teens and twenties. He was 'in love' but no-one seemed to be quite right until he met Olivia and then something seemed to change very quickly. They have both described about 'just knowing' the other was the person they wanted to share the rest of their lives with. I think Olivia unlocked something in Matthew, which meant he was able to let go of the very special place Abi had held in his heart.

In so many ways, Matthew is 'Jack the lad': full of bluster, game for a laugh, always the centre of the action. But inside he is a very tender-hearted person who is hugely emotional and who keeps the area of his life which is connected with his feelings about Abi so very private. I think many of his friends might get a real shock if they knew about it. And, of course, if any of them read this, they will. But their experience of him is different from mine, I know things they don't and perhaps actually it will make things fall into place.

I found it very sad as we talked, that Matthew has what appears to be so few memories of Abi. He has a remarkable memory for so many things. The thing he wants most in life, to remember more about his little sister, he can't have because he has shut it out. Yet I know how this feels, sometimes I can only remember the pain. I have to force myself to remember the happy times, actively take myself back to the day she was born and how happy I felt then. And then I remember other occasions when she and I were together. I remember breastfeeding her in the middle of the night, it was very cold in our bedroom in Dundee and the two of us would be tucked up in bed together whilst Paddy slept on, oblivious, beside me. I remember the times we all went on holidays, pushing her in her push-chair or carrying her on our shoulders. I rmember just being around her, feeding her – because she had a great appetite and enjoyed her food as most Neligans do!

As time has moved on, Matthew and Olivia now have three sons, Henry, James and Louis, who have all been such a wonderful addition to the family. They are brilliant parents, both of them are very sensible and don't seem to panic about minor ailments, and they are able to work out together what needs to happen if one of the boys is unwell. All three boys have contributed hugely to the healing process of everyone in the family. My father commented after Henry was born how people's faces changed when they held him, and what a great healing influence he was.

A further positive aspect has been that Matthew and Olivia have talked to their children about Abi, and Henry has begun to ask some questions about her in the direct way that young children do. Matthew appears to be coping well with this. He has also contributed to this book by creating the family tree explaining who is who.

Overall, I think the way in which he and I went into this together was cathartic, useful and filled in some of the gaps we both had. Olivia has read this and I hope this enables her to feel she knows more about us and our history.

Six

Cathy

Cathy is a tall, blonde, elegant and intelligent young woman, who looks far younger than her years. From being quite a small child she wanted to have a little sister. When Simon was born and Paddy told Matthew and her that the new baby had arrived and they had a little brother, she flung herself down on the bed and thumped the covers, saying, "It's not, it's a girl, it's a girl". She took refuge for a while with an imaginary friend, who went to playschool with her, although it's

Cathy holding Abi close

interesting that her friend was a little boy called Peter. So to lose her first little sister in 1980 when she was five was hard, though looking back I am not sure how much she really understood. She knows it did happen, but can't recall anything about that time. Abi's birth was, I think, exciting for her. She had a little sister to fuss over, and I think she imagined the future as they grew up together.

They were just about to share a room together: a big gap of six years between the girls meant that Simon and Abi had shared a room for quite a while. Cathy was looking forward to her 'turn' in having Abi to herself. I think they managed just one or two nights before Abi was taken ill. It was only years later that I remembered even Cathy (and I mean along with myself and I guess Paddy too) had blamed herself somehow for her death. It's only been through this process that I have understood this was because Cathy had been unwell with a cold for a few days before Abi became ill too. She thought she had given her the cold, and that had infected Abi in such a way that she had died.

Cathy had a tempestuous childhood and adolescence; from being a small child she had a very strong mind of her own and a temper to go with it! One day, when she was aged about three or four we were going for a family walk together. We thought it wasn't a good idea for her to take her doll's pushchair with her and a tussle began between her and Paddy. They argued so much that in the end she managed to break the pushchair in her efforts to hang on to it and take it with her.

Her teenage years were difficult, often punctuated by crying fits and her seeming very unhappy. She took refuge in her work, determined to achieve and do as well as Matthew had done. She took on more and more and got excellent results at GCSE and A Level. But she wasn't happy. I made allowances for her over and over again, and, looking back, it must have driven the boys mad. And she drove me mad sometimes too. I could be patient and understanding for so long, but then I used to flip and would feel unable to cope any longer. I couldn't keep on being understanding so I would end up having my own tantrum and needing Paddy to come and sort things out. All in all, we had some difficult times and I am sure we could have handled things better.

At University, Cathy took advantage of the free counselling services and that experience helped her to understand what her feelings in relation to Abi were about and, I think, to come to some kind of resolution. Periodically she has accessed counselling again and this has enabled her to have further understanding and work more fully through the process. It's also meant that we are able to talk about Abi far more readily than I can with either of the boys. For me that has meant I have found her the easiest person to talk to, apart from Paddy.

Cathy was the first person I interviewed for this book and it was easy: we weren't aware of where the time had gone. I found it really helpful – the questions seemed to flow and though she was upset from time to time, it didn't seem to halt the conversation we had. I noticed when I was transcribing this that I was in it and out of it at the same time. I was able to hear the questions I asked and notice that they had a kind of objectivity about them – but also there were times when I know I felt defensive inside about things I had done or said, or not.

I started by asking if the way to begin was to talk about memories – what happened.

"My memories have changed over time, or rather as I've been given more information. I think my memories are quite strong and quite accurate. The actual couple of days when she was in hospital are quite strong. I remember the Thursday morning, you were at the hospital and Dad was talking about going to visit whilst we were eating breakfast. I said, 'What about school?' Dad said no school today and that was the first time I realised it was serious because we were being allowed a day off school. It meant that Abi didn't just have a cold. It really shocked me as we were never allowed a day off school."

Do you remember anything about what Dad had said to you?

"I remember the day before she went into hospital. You had picked us up from school, walking down that little road towards school to meet us, you were carrying her as she was quite ill and distressed, and you said you would have to take her to hospital as she wasn't getting better. She was red in the face. My next memory is of Dad saying that at breakfast – a gap of two days. Simon went to judo on Tuesday evening. I remember being in the hospital visiting and standing round the bed – Granny, Grandpa and Granny Nel being there. I remember her having 'crybaby' with her and us all standing round the bed. The only other thing I remember is the doctors coming in and telling us she was brain dead and then you and Dad going back in before they turned off the machines."

You must have gone home then.

"I remember being with Granny Ash and talking to her and me saying it was my fault as I'd been ill – I felt bad as I'd had the same thing before her. Granny Ash dismissed it straight away – said it wasn't my fault and I think I accepted that."

You were only nine.

"That night, Granny Nel drove me and Matthew to take me to ballet class but we couldn't find the place. I can't really believe that happened. Matthew tried to help us find the way but we never got to ballet that night; we found the right area but not the church hall so we just came back. Glad I didn't end up there, it was bad enough going to dancing normally! I used to end up in tears after ballet most times anyway but it did give us something to do, driving round in the dark.

When I went back to school, my teacher had told everyone in the year so I wouldn't have to tell people. I guess Dad did it to make sure people knew. It was good and bad as some people shouldn't have known, there were some nasty girls who said things to me. Just once..."

(Cathy began crying at the memory of this.)

"They said I didn't deserve a sister, I was having a fight or argument with a girl I didn't really like but I don't really remember the context and I can't remember how long afterwards it happened."

What a cruel thing to say, so what did you do?

"I can't remember. I don't think I had any comeback. It must have been the same year."

Have you thought about it a lot? Do you know what stopped you from telling me things like that?

"I didn't want to upset you, but it wasn't just things like that. For a long time I felt I couldn't talk about Abi as you'd get upset."

Were you trying to protect me?

"Yes."

(Though she didn't sound sure about that.)

"I knew you would get upset other times anyway, and I didn't want to make it an extra time."

We were all upset inside all the time anyway, and that upset feeling might come out as crying or being angry or whatever.

"You don't think like that as a child. Lots of things happened at school I didn't tell you about – nasty things people would say and do. Not necessarily connected with Abi dying though.

I think you did the right thing by telling the teacher then because I didn't have to have any awkward conversations – so it was the right thing to do. Later when people have had friends who've died, I've only recently managed to get over that awkwardness."

Do you think you know what to say to people now?

"Not really but I just think you have to say something: like say, 'Sorry about your Mum'. Especially if it's someone you don't know well, just to try and support them – quite a few friends have had grandparents die – sometimes they've been very ill. It is easier with someone you are closer to."

Have you ever come across someone else who's had a brother or sister die?

"Yes, but not the same circumstances as me. A boyfriend had a younger brother who lived for just a few days after he was born. He was about two so he didn't remember. We would talk about it, but it wasn't like me, it was a different experience. He always said if that baby had lived he wouldn't have had his sister. I'm close to people whose mums have died. That made us closer even though it was quite a different experience."

Do you think it's given you more understanding of what it's like to be bereaved, to grieve, to understand the stages people go through?

"Yes, but it's quite pessimistic in a way because it's 20 years ago and I'm still grieving. I find it very hard with someone who's newly bereaved to say that you'll never get over it, nothing will ever be the same again, you won't feel alive again, you won't ever get over it. That is not what they want to hear. I feel a bit of a separation. Also every loss is different: a grandfather who has been really ill for a long time and then dies might feel like a relief. The natural order is that the old people should die and that's very different from your mum dying, or your sibling or your child. Or a very different view after a long illness, or very suddenly; or if you aren't close to a grandparent.

Every single person's relationship is so different. That is why I find it so awkward knowing what to say as I find that people can be so crass. I feel so sensitive to what I say, in case it's the wrong thing. Every person they meet asking them if they are OK. They might be going to the pub for a quiet drink and then being made to go through things again. I don't necessarily want to remind them or needing to put a brave face on it to acquaintances. Saying, 'It's OK, never mind', but, actually, it isn't OK but you don't want to break down in public."

That's something you've noticed about your friends now, but your experience is 20 years ago, and your only other close experience of death since then has been Granny Nel then. That is a different experience, but I just wonder if you would say you are still grieving for Granny now?

"No, but I grieved more than I expected to. It's seven years ago now, it was when I was 22. I'd say the grief was completely different, it felt natural. The main thing about Abi was it felt like everything had been turned upside down, nothing was normal again. Not true with Granny at all. The way she died was in the best possible way she could have done. I was surprised I still went through all the same kind of things, like the anger. I'd get very angry reading obituaries about people who died at 95 – angry that other people had longer when she was so fit. Lots of times I was just caught by surprise, it came out of the blue and I felt very upset and really missed her.

I wish I'd spent more time with her as an adult to understand her more. One of the last times I saw her, it must have been her 80th birthday, we were getting food at Dave and Pam's and she made a point of singling me out, saying, 'You must come and sit with me'. It was so different and she was interested in me. I'd never felt that before and wished I'd had more moments with her when we could have appreciated each other.

Other friends had grandparents die and I was quite wary of what to say to them, my boyfriend was very dismissive when Granny died and he didn't realise it was a big deal. But there was a lot going on for him at the time anyway. He couldn't work out why I was so upset. Though I think it was a combination of things: having just got my degree, moving house in Leeds and so on. Everything felt wonderful and then I just came crashing down when I heard she had died."

100

Any other memories from the time when Abi died?

"Vague ones of her funeral, sitting in the room and it all being very white. Another vague one of her memorial service at 126; the vicar next door who said something. So many people crammed in, sitting on the floor. I don't remember specific people but I was sitting next to Simon and I know you asked us to read something. It wasn't particularly appropriate; it had no real resonance or significance because it wasn't about death or about Abi. It was just a children's poem. A nice poem, maybe just one that we liked."

Your Dad and I always sang songs to you all at bedtime to get you off to sleep. You could each choose a song every evening, and you all had different favourites from time to time. At the meeting to celebrate Abi's life, we wanted people to join in with the singing but I now realise that was quite a challenge given that there was such an air of sadness in the room, as well as lots of little children around who could potentially pop up with any kind of direct question.

(Cathy and I had quite a discussion trying to remember the songs we sang; exactly what those songs were. I sang one of them which lightened the tone in the room as we were talking.)

"Thinking about Granny's memorial – it was really nice and helpful; a good way to remember her and talk about her. I don't remember much about Abi's – it strikes me that we were all such a big mess of shock and emotion – maybe a year after rather than a week after would have been better. But I've just thought of that now. I understand why you had it then, funerals are a way of saying goodbye – but I don't know that we were ready to say goodbye."

I've thought about this since, and perhaps it was too soon, before we had really had time to think about what we wanted. I think we just wanted to get things over with as soon as we could, plus Christmas was approaching and we didn't want things to get mixed up with that. I think the shock was so overwhelming that we made lots of decisions that in retrospect we would not have done if we had given ourselves just a little more time to think about it.

Can you remember anything about how you and Matthew and Simon related to each other?

"Not really, though I remember we all slept in the same room that night. Remembering, the relationships have become all mixed up. Certain things I remember doing but I don't know how old I was or how often, if it happened all the time or if it happened once, or all the time for one year or ten years. I wouldn't be able to say if things changed after she died. Before she died, I was very jealous of Matthew and Simon and their relationship with Abi; I felt left out. They both got on much better than I did with her. I had to try and put on an act; it didn't feel like a natural relationship. I felt that a lot anyway.

I'd say let's play this or let's do this but maybe she wasn't interested. Then I'd have to think of something else and try and be cool. Matthew and Simon just barged in and she loved the rough and tumble whilst I wanted to do girly things. One thing I remember is that photo of her doing the splits, the one where I'm holding her legs and of me doing that with her."

As we look at the photo again now, I wonder if Abi looks a bit long-suffering and if she is thinking, 'Let's just get the photo over and done with' and you are clinging on to her and won't let go!

**Cathy's pride in Abi's
ability to stretch her legs!**

*"I remember doing it and I thought it was amazing she
could do it. I wasn't that bendy (despite doing ballet)
but she wasn't that interested in doing it. I forced her
into playing a game she didn't really want to do. I was
desperate for her to like me.*

*What I remember (and is this true of all two year olds?) is
that she just wanted to run around, getting into mischief.
So did the other two. I was more introspective. I was
getting interested in how I looked; obviously the boys just
didn't care about that kind of thing. The extension of that
is that I had this little sister. We used to dress the same
sometimes, it wasn't like she was a doll, but a bit like
that. Dressing her up, playing with her, I wasn't reacting
with her as a person. More like a live doll! Not an idea I
like at all."*

How did Abi's death affect you and your relationships?

"In lots of ways, but it's hard to put your finger on them. I look back and see tensions, us seeking attention because Abi died. I don't think we felt as secure as we had done, or didn't get as much attention. Matthew acting up; me striving to get high marks at school. It became more and more of a big deal to come top, and if I didn't, I pretended I didn't care. I was bothered even though I pretended I wasn't. I wanted to be magnanimous and pleased if one of my friends came above me."

I always thought it was primarily about your relationship with Matthew, but as you are talking I realise this isn't the whole picture.

"I wanted to be best at everything. I wanted to be top, the best in the class. That was important because I couldn't beat Matthew. I made lists in my head, I couldn't think of anything I beat him in – sport, music, schoolwork – there was nothing that I could do better than him. Nothing I could say was solely mine; that I was better at than him. Abi's death accentuated it definitely. Work was a way of being good, being top, and I knew you would be proud of me if I did well."

So did you work hard to please me and Dad?

"No, it was much more for me. I couldn't have kept it up that long just to please you. This is a complex thing I've not worked out fully. Partly it was me wanting to be perfect. To be really good, so I wouldn't be punished again."

So you view Abi's death as a punishment? Or was working hard a protection against bad things happening?

"No, it was a bad thing that happened and I didn't want any other bad things to happen. I put all my energy into my work. The messages from school and you and Dad were to work hard and do well academically and everything will be OK; it will lead to you being successful. Success equals happiness. Get a good job. It wasn't about protection, but be good and I will be rewarded and things will work out for the best. It wasn't true; it didn't work that way at all. I was a bit disappointed about that!"

Were you cross?

"I was disillusioned that academic success doesn't count for anything: having an outgoing personality and having confidence would have stood me in better stead at University. For me everything is linked to academic success. A close friend says this too about me, that my self-worth is wrapped up in academic success."

To what extent did her death affect your life, your beliefs about yourself, and other people?

"It has completely transformed the way I think about things, in as much as a nine year old had worked things out about life and so on. Before she died, I'd have assembly every day at school, say prayers there, I'd go to church with Brownies too. I've not thought about it deeply but before then I believed in God. All of that came from school. Things were different at home, I think more deeply wrapped up with belief in authority: in medicine, power, the police, the government, those people were there and everything would turn out for the best. Bad things don't happen to good people. I had belief as a child. Faith in religion; I remember praying when she was ill that she would get better."

Did you pray before?

"Can't remember; I'm not sure. As soon as she died, it was black and white. I had prayed for her to get better and she didn't, therefore God doesn't exist – it was that quick. I've no flicker of religious belief now. Life is random; things happen for no reason."

What do you believe now, what happens when people die?

"Nothing."

An afterlife?

"No, my idea of an afterlife is that you live on in people's memories of you, things you've done. It's not traditional, but I draw some comfort from that. I believe in fate a bit; more just that things will happen and you've no control over them, not that there's something or someone else pulling the strings. What happens to you, you can't control. I spent a lot of time wondering why she died, what it means. When I talked to Dorothy Rowe[13] she asked me what you had told me about the facts of what happened. I said you had given a bowdlerised version, then later on you told me in detail what happened. She asked about why it happened and what you said."

The bigger why?

"Yes that's it. Don't know if I ever asked, I don't remember."

Why do you think it happened?

---

[13] Dorothy Rowe, psychologist and author, interviewed Cathy a few years ago for a book she was writing on the relationships between brothers and sisters.

"I don't think there is a bigger why, I don't think there is an answer. The conversation I had with Dorothy Rowe was about wondering if these things are to test us, God's time for us to be tested in whatever ways that might be. I think anything like that is unhelpful. The balancing question is, 'Why not then?' I could have done quite well if Abi had stayed alive; I didn't need this test in this way, thanks very much."

One thing I've drawn from it is that if she hadn't died, I wouldn't be doing the work I do, nor writing this. This seems something positive to draw from it rather than living a whole life of negativity and pessimism.

"I wouldn't be the person I am if she hadn't died; I could be a much better, much nicer person. I do spend quite a lot of time wondering what she would be like and I tend to go the devil's advocate route. We would probably argue a lot – I can't project magical qualities onto her."

Do you think you did that?

"I think I did do that for a long time. At University the counsellor picked up that I compared myself to her, and Matthew. All these wonderful things about her, but you can't be jealous of a two year old because all two year olds are wonderful. Then they grow up and would be different. It's not a fair comparison to make. That really helped. I realised a lot of things I wanted for myself: I was jealous of her for being bubbly; everyone loved her. She was very friendly and she had a lust for life. I projected those things onto an adult or teenage version of her. I thought she would have had loads of friends but that's not necessarily true. She has no adult anxieties or neuroses; she doesn't have bad moods, PMT. But that's because she is stuck as a little child.

It hit me last year at college when I made friends with people the same age as she would have been. One friend, in particular, is just one month's difference from Abi's age (as she would have been) and she's quite similar to me in a lot of ways, stubborn and loses her temper.

For a while I was thinking that my relationship with her was seen through a mirror of Abi as well. She always forgets I'm older than her and so do I, I think I'm 23 too! I think in quite a detached way, what would my relationship with Abi be like now if she was 22? Hard to imagine now. It wasn't such a big jump when she could have been nine or ten. She could have done anything, anything could have happened to her. It was nice but also upsetting too."

Do you think she got stuck in a time warp as a perfect little person?

"It's hard for me, she was stuck in that time warp and I mustn't compare myself to her."

Who helped, was there anyone who stood out? Or has it just been an internal process for you to help yourself?

"The counsellor at University helped. But that was me working it out, she facilitated it. My friend whose mum died helped because she was going through a similar thing. We were in a similar position and most other friends didn't have that kind of experience. It was quite isolating. No-one understood – for me and then for her too. So I think we helped each other. We had a pretty good idea what it was like for the other one. So it's been people outside the family, including my boyfriend at University.

I've only recently worked it out that I've spent a lot of time searching for a sisterly figure, a best friend figure.

I've asked myself what it was that led me to need such an intense friendship with my best friend when I was at school. For three or four years we were very, very close and didn't have many other friends. Between about 12 to 15 we spent all our time together. We had a secret language, little nicknames etc. I've wondered why I needed that, and then it was taken away when she got a boyfriend.

I do feel I have close friendships now, but not that I come first and can ring them up any time. I've had that with boyfriends when we were going out, and even after that too. We'd still meet up and go for lunch or a gallery. I felt a bit needy. And I felt jealous of people who had that best friend relationship, something that I really want. I've found it difficult when friends have boyfriends and put them before me. I wonder if it's because I feel the gap and something missing. I've always felt that there's a gap but I feel it less now: it used to be an Abi-shaped gap, but it has changed. It moved to a best friend shaped type of gap, and now it's a boyfriend shaped gap. A relationship with one boyfriend in particular was helpful, I felt very loved and wanted and much more secure. Though it was a difficult time when I was going out with him.

When I was 14, I did an English project about memory. I was interviewing various people and asking Simon what his saddest memory was. He couldn't stop crying and couldn't speak. He was only about 11 then. I didn't talk about emotional things with my brothers anyway. I'd talk to you, not directly about Abi, but about other things which got stirred up as a result of that."

Were there any creative things that helped – books, poems, music, art?

"Certain songs I couldn't listen to without crying, so not a help, really. One problem is that by the time I was getting to process it all, I was a teenager and having all those hormones and moods. Being into goth music, Sylvia Plath and listening to depressing music didn't help matters much! I wouldn't say I'd used any of those things to help me with my feelings about Abi. If I feel upset I might read Jeeves and Wooster to take my mind off things, but not this."

It can be the other way round, though; I can listen to really sad music if I want to make myself sad.

"I don't do that, but there was a song by REM called 'Losing my Religion', which is why it has that resonance. The lyrics are quite depressing. It was played at 'Spiders'[14] and I had to get my boyfriend to bring me home. It still reminds me but I can control it and wouldn't have to leave somewhere if it was playing now."

Has it got easier over time telling friends?

"Even more difficult in a different way. I find it very, very hard to tell people. Going to Japan, then University, then Japan again, I made many new sets of friends. How do I tell friends when I've known them for a long time? People don't know what to do with it. It feels like it becomes a big deal. I remember sitting one guy down after a year or so and telling him, he didn't really know what to do with it. It had got to the point where I couldn't just drop it into the conversation.

"It was a similar thing when I did my Master's. It's not more difficult emotionally, it doesn't upset me every day; it's more the logistics of how to do it. If I couldn't get out

---

[14] Spiders is a nightclub in Hull.

110

of bed because of the depressions I used to have, my housemates would want to know what the matter was, so in a way that was easier because it was very hard to avoid. If I become good friends with people, I'd like them to know but I can't slip it into the conversation. But you don't want to say as soon as you meet someone. It is a bit of a conversation killer anyway. I mention brothers – people ask about sisters."

So how do you cope with those awkward questions?

"Usually I say, 'No, I don't have any sisters'. I wish I had the courage to say yes, but I've never ever said it to anyone. I have sometimes said yes when I knew it wasn't going to go any further or changed the subject. I ended up telling two people the day we got our results, because one of them had failed. We were talking about the worst thing that had ever happened to each of us. Not a good situation to be telling them this! I felt bad, because I'd said my situation was worse than theirs. But then who am I to say this is worse than your situation?"

Do you think it is the worst thing that can happen to anyone?

"It's the worst thing that's happened to me. Maybe it depends how old you are. I think if I'd been older it wouldn't have been so bad, my personality would have been more formed so it might not have affected me as much. I sometimes wonder about people who have had older siblings die, at least you know them as a person who has the world ahead of themselves, you know them as a fully formed personality. I don't know if it makes it worse."

Maybe it just makes it different.

"I've not solved the problem of when to tell people – maybe it's best to mention it in passing straight away. Matthew has a picture of her in his wallet, I don't know how much he is asked – but people can ask about it. I don't carry one round. I had one framed by my bed for a long time and sometimes people would ask about that. And I had a lot of photos on my wall including some of Abi. People in Japan asked but I didn't want to get into it."

How did you explain all that to Koichi[15]?

"I've no memories of having that conversation but I was on anti-depressants when I met him and I couldn't hide that from him. He was very anti that and concerned anyway so I tried to describe things in simple terms. I don't remember telling him about Abi. There are some people I'm close to that I still haven't told but want to. It was her birthday when I was away in New Zealand with Steph, and I just didn't know how to broach it. Broaching is the difficult part, once I've done it I can talk about her more naturally in conversations."

I remembered reading about the writer Alice Thomas Ellis and a statement she made which was, "I am the mother of seven children, five of whom are living". I had said something similar in a residential group in Tuscany, and making that statement was a first for me. "I'm the mother of five children, three of whom are alive and well. Two of my daughters have died." It was a big deal for me at the time saying it in a group; it did feel a bit false and it was hard, but I guess that was because it was a new experience for me, so quite a test really. I think I am more able to weave it in when I meet people but I'm in a different kind of group and context to the places you find yourself.

---

[15]   Koichi was a Japanese boyfriend of Cathy's.

"People who've had a parent die are asked about their parents and it's fine to say different things about families. They don't presume that you've had a sibling die; it's like not assuming people do or don't have children themselves. Asking those kinds of questions can be just a conversation filler trying to get to know someone, but you don't necessarily want someone to know everything about you. One step forward for me if someone asks me directly would be to say yes. You just might kill it dead, you don't want to say, 'She died 20 years ago but I'm fine now, don't worry about it'. You can be flippant and mention silly things in passing, but not the first time as you sound so uncaring! It is an ongoing dilemma really. Boyfriends are much easier because they see photos and we spend much more time getting to know one another."

Is there anything you would have liked to have done but didn't? Like marking her birthday or the anniversary of her death?

"I would have done but I felt it was a taboo subject. Felt I couldn't suggest anything. There was nowhere we could go; there was no grave. I think I'd have liked to have gone somewhere to think about her and talk, just the five of us. I'd like to toast her and have a drink for her. Sometimes I've done it with friends."

Is there anywhere special to go that feels connected with Abi for you?

"Not really, though we could have created somewhere. In the recent aftermath, there must have been places that we would have visited with her when she was alive – the Humber Bridge or Pearson Park. I associate nature with people who have gone, particularly Granny; I guess because it's peaceful. More the feeling I get when I'm

113

outdoors; being able more to think about those people, less distraction. When I am in a park I can think more about people who aren't there, even if it's noisy."

Do those people feel closer to you when you do that?

"Yes, it's more I can have an uninterrupted think about them. I don't feel their presence, but because I am able to think undisturbed, I can get closer to how I feel."

Have you ever felt her presence with you?

"No, but just after she died, with the two doors into the sitting room at 126, I saw her coming through one of the doors just out of the corner of my eye – more like false memory."

Perhaps...

"I think I would have liked us to have created some kind of ritual so that even if we weren't all living together we could gather and sit and think and maybe talk about her. Maybe if we all did that at the same time it might be helpful to us all. One year a friend gave me a card when we were having a party on Abi's birthday. It made a big difference to me to know that someone else knew about it and remembered."

Do you wish we had done something to remember Abi, or that there was a grave or somewhere significant to visit?

"Yes or something like that. I suppose we have a tree, but it would be good to have somewhere else we can go. It doesn't have to have associations with Abi, but just getting out of our normal lives and thinking about her. It might be an artificial creation, but it would be helpful, I think."

What have been the worst times? Are there any that stand out? Were there any depths of despair for you? When did they occur?

"Every six months really, it's not just about Abi, it's about having lost her and the effect it had on my life, how that influenced my teenage years, things that happen now – all three get mixed together. Sometimes it's not about being sad about Abi, I'm sad for me as a little girl, sorry for myself as a child. I think it's odd. I'm a different person. No time is particularly bad because of the way things have got mixed up."

How about going to Japan, did that help?

"Yes in lots of ways. The first time I went was when I was 18, and because I was away from Matthew, I didn't have to compare myself to him and I felt independent. Then with you being pregnant when I was there, it was difficult that I was away, but at least the positive thing was that it allowed me to let go of that hope of having another brother or sister. I'd been holding onto that till then. When I found out you were pregnant, I was so happy and everything seemed wonderful; another brother or sister to take the pain away. When you miscarried it felt like coming back to normal, down-to-earth. That hope was unrealistic, it always was. The whole nine years I'd been hoping had been unrealistic. It shocked me out of thinking that way. It's not going to happen, so draw a line under it. One good thing was that I was with a friend and we were close, so living together I felt day to day secure in that friendship."

I had no idea that you were holding onto that hope just like I did for all that time.

"When I went back to Japan after my degree, I was feeling stronger because I'd had a lot of counselling and I had a new boyfriend shortly before I went away. I felt much more secure. It was hard being in Japan and away from home. There were difficulties with the long-distance relationship as well, and sometimes I felt very lonely. When the job was terrible, it felt to be external things, rather than depression from within. I grew up quite a lot while there, got more settled in myself. I gained an ability to make friends and talk to people. Since then, other counselling I've had wasn't talking about Abi much. I've felt fairly static in my feelings – not much more to work through; just time spent with it. I still revisit the same feelings, being angry – it feels less raw now. 20 years and still not over it. It might not happen as often but when I do get upset, it's still the same feelings. I get so angry about how unfair it was, it shouldn't have happened, we didn't deserve it."

That's the thing that you can't really say to people when they are newly bereaved – about it being 20 years on and still feeling the same to a great extent at times.

"I never forget about her – people say time heals etc. I don't think you want to hear that – it might betray them. Sometimes I feel that I've betrayed her, because I can't remember much about her."

If you'd been able to read something at the time that told you that other people still feel as raw and angry years after the event and it's OK because it's all part of the process, would that have been helpful?

"I think so – being angry is one of the stages. Reading about it can seem clinical. Passed that stage etc. I realised that it's a cyclical rather than linear process. It's hard to deal with people who don't seem to be that bothered – I

116

had a friend whose mum died, she didn't show it at all. I remember telling her to be angry and be a bitch, stop being so accommodating and looking after other people: 'Your mum died just a year ago!' – but it wasn't her way of dealing with it. Everyone's grief is so individual – anything you read could so easily be crass.

There are two options. One is to pretty things up i.e. 'Everything will be all right' but it's a massive understatement and it's not true. The other is that it will always be really hard – it's a desperate thing to hear. Really hard."

But there is a middle ground: "This is what it was like for me, and my husband, my daughter, my sons". We all have different kinds of stories, but my guess is there will be some themes and overlaps. I found it helped me a lot to read about people's real experiences. I got every book I could find out of the library – I scoured the shelves.

"Things are only helpful after the fact – the first few months or years you won't take it in. I've not read that much about bereavement – not in the first person anyway."

Did your counsellor talk about it?

"I read it in magazines and things."

What do you think about me writing this? You said at first it was a good idea.

"It was my idea wasn't it, for you to get on with the writing? 'When are you going to write your book, Mum?'"

Is there anything you would like me to include? Anything to come back to? What thoughts have you had about where it goes and what happens to it?

"That's quite hard to answer – till I've read it. We've an unusual name, so anyone reading it will know it's me. I have wondered about how it would be if a lot of people who don't know me read a lot of very emotional stuff about my inner life, my depression and so on – I want to choose who knows that. Not something I think you can predict. You don't know – if you publish this, it could become very popular – widely read – I'd be constantly meeting people – everyone would know stuff about me I didn't want them to know; them judging me because they have information.

I think that tangible thing is really important – something shared – it's been very isolating. It would be a nice thing for us to have.

Some of what I've said – death is a conversation killer. I've pretended not to see someone, or felt uncomfortable contacting someone because I know they've just been bereaved. There should be more openness about death and how people have felt. I'd like a return to that society where people talk about it, and it isn't a taboo subject.

The blurb about Victorian authors: everything they wrote about death and it being commonplace to lose babies and young children. It's not like that now: so it must be very hard for people who've had babies who have died. They must think about who do we tell, how do we process it, and make it acceptable for others. Our family has all struggled with those things: other people have struggled with it too – it all seems unfair.

A wider audience – could be liberating. It would make it easier to talk about it because this book could push us all into that situation and we would have to face it head on. I'm not sure if we are all comfortable with doing that."

The process of time might allow the family to be more open. Particularly if they read it, have the chance to give their opinion and so on, and also it may depend on how I've written it. I hope it will be sensitive to everyone's views, but it is important it's honest at the same time, otherwise what's the point? I want people to grasp the wide range of experiences, feelings, understanding and so on. If I edit what I include that won't really be a help to anyone.

"You were a fully formed individual – your life has changed dramatically, so has mine because I was only nine. My life would have changed anyway. She affected my whole childhood, made me the person I am now and it still affects me. Do I want to have children or not? Part of me really wants to; another part thinks I would never dare. Is that just trying to replace her? If something happened, I wouldn't be able to cope.

I've no sense of the bigger question of why. I don't think she had a destiny: she came for whatever; she had a big influence on me in every way, but so have my brothers! I used to think that as a child and a teenager – why give her to us if she was just going to be taken away. I don't believe in any of that now. To teach us what love was – I think all that is nonsense. Platitudes again!"

She was a big influence, but we maybe put too much onto it because she has died.

"The experience formed my personality and attitudes to life – everyone else did too of course but in smaller and more gradual ways – that was so cataclysmic and sudden. So unnatural; so against everything. It affected and changed the way I think about life."

Does that make you sad?

"Very depressed sometimes, I feel like there's no point to anything, no meaning to life and the only way to cope is to be busy and distract myself. If I keep busy I'll stop being depressed. That's a game I play. So I go round in circles. Nothing anyone can say to me, but maybe if I have children of my own that will make me think there is some purpose. I felt it was proved so strongly that there isn't a purpose – things like that can just happen. I suppose there is some meaning in the idea of the family."

It was our idea to have Abi, if the baby before had not died she wouldn't have been born. We planned our family and our plan worked up till the time at which that baby died, then we had to have a massive re-think about whether we wanted to take the risk again. The desire to have a big family was a huge one for both of us, so it was a very big deal to take that risk again and go through another pregnancy. It wasn't just the emotional aspect of another pregnancy; there was the physical side too for me. It was a big challenge to face another nine months of pregnancy when the last one had ended in our baby dying. But all of that was worth it for me; I would have done anything to have another healthy child.

Dad and I tried to create our own meaning, the family was and is so important to both of us; the act of creating our family, bringing you up in the way which we felt was right – which very much mirrored how we had both been brought up. Now I see the values and principles you three live by, the way in which Matthew and Olivia are bringing up their boys, the partners you have each chosen and I feel very proud that you seem to be on the same wavelength as Dad and I. What you talk about as being important is what we think too – and about some things

I think you are even stronger in your views than we are, which is wonderful. I wonder what it would be like if you had rejected our values and were very materialistic and commercially-minded?

"Family is very important to me too, there is some meaning in my life there. But it can be taken away just like that, I can't rely on that, can't hold onto it, it's not enough. Anyone else can go at any time. What would have happened if one of us had died as a teenager?"

I thought about that a lot and sometimes I got very anxious, particularly when you were beginning to cycle to school and then later learning to drive and going out in the car on your own. To some extent I still worry about it. I think the gap years you took probably helped because I realised you were doing all kinds of things far away which I didn't know about. It was no good me worrying about 'what might be happening' because I didn't know what you were doing in Japan and I couldn't influence you at all at such a distance. There was a stage when I had to really control myself not to ask Matthew to ring me when he got back to London having visited us at home. The anxieties have abated somewhat but they still surface at times. I don't want to be a clingy mother, but I had to work very hard while you were growing up to let go and it was really difficult. I know that all mothers have to do it so I don't know if it was different, or if I bent over backwards.

"We children weren't that aware at the time – it was just on you and Dad, it didn't have that big effect on the family – we didn't really know."

After Cathy and I had finished our conversation, I realised that I had had some of my thoughts and questions answered but it had also raised areas for me which I hadn't known about.

I realised that Cathy's thoughts about her being to blame for Abi's death weren't dismissed as suddenly as I had thought at the time. I had imagined that when we explained about why Abi had died, that was enough. Perhaps we didn't say enough, or didn't come back to it at a later point to make sure the children understood why she had died. Cathy kept her thoughts to herself and it took a long time for her to understand and accept that she wasn't to blame.

When she told me about the unkind child at school taunting her, I felt as I did when Cathy was a little girl and wanted to protect her. I felt angry all over again with the girls who were unkind to her then. It is only through this process that I've understood that each of the children had experienced at least one situation when they got very upset about something someone said to them at school. If I did know at the time, I've blotted it out. It makes me wonder about how we educate our children. What would help in schools when those kinds of situations happen to children? Or is it just part of the process of growing up and through something like this, needing to find your own response and way of coping?

I think, overall, our children's schools were very helpful and thoughtful. Certainly the way in which they made sure that their schoolmates knew about what had happened, so that our children didn't have to tell their friends about Abi dying, was very useful. My guess is that for teachers, just as much as everyone else we came into contact with, they did what they felt was right at the time, but the most important thing was to put the situation into the past and move on into the future.

Our conversation reminded me again of the cherry blossom tree that Paddy's mum gave us after Abi died. We moved the tree to two different houses, but once we left Hull completely we didn't take it with us. I didn't want the effort of moving a well-established tree and finding that it had died. I preferred the memory of how it blossomed around her birthday and looked so lovely then. As the tree matured, it naturally became even more beautiful. One of my last memories of it was how it looked when Abi would have been 13 and on the brink of becoming a woman.

As I read again and think about the conversation Cathy and I had then, I feel very proud that she has the insight she has, but our conversation was some time ago and things have moved on hugely. She is married now and talking about having children and it seems important to her that she has them. I think the fears she has have abated to some extent, but I am basing that on the fact that she hasn't talked about them so I realise they may be there still.

She is a wonderful daughter; she is great company and has a talent for being able to burst my bubble when it needs bursting. By that I mean the times when I worry needlessly about things to do, or people who are stressed. She loves being with Henry, James and Louis; she has lots of patience and seems very calm when she is looking after them. They have been such a healing addition to the family. I think they have been a catalyst in helping Cathy and her husband, Simon, realise that parenthood is something they can aim for and will enjoy.

Seven

Simon

Simon is the most difficult of my children to describe in a sentence or two. He is a complex individual, talented musically, possessed of great intelligence, good-looking and thoughtful and kind as well as able to be self-centred and critical of himself and others. I think he plumbs the depths of my love for him, by which I mean I feel a physical hurt when our relationship is going through a rocky patch. The relationship feels much more challenging than the relationship I have with my other two.

I felt anxious about talking to Simon, I think partly because I wondered how much he would remember and because our relationship had been through a difficult patch not long before we had our conversation. I should have remembered that this is the chap with a fantastic memory, who could recount films and books in incredible detail when he was a child. So the number of memories that he had and the clarity of them shouldn't really have surprised me that much. We spent a good time together although I think he was nervous, and sounded a bit dubious about what we might be talking about.

I started by saying that when I have been talking to the family, whilst it has been emotional, it has helped. We have laughed a lot and people have been able to talk about their memories. It brought things back for everyone.

I asked him what memories he had, given that he was so young (only six) when Abi died. That could mean that you have a very different take on it to the others. Can you remember anything about it?

"Yes, I remember the night she went into hospital, the pyjamas she was wearing, and going to visit her."

Do you think you remember it because of going to judo?

"It's just the pyjamas – my old ones with 'hot shot' on them. You or Dad was holding her and I didn't think much of it at that time – that she was going to hospital. I'd been in hospital with my hernia when I was younger – not normal, but I thought, off she goes and I'll see her later. It is just the fact of her wearing my old pyjamas that I remember. I remember visiting her in hospital, the slippers and blue gowns we had to put on before we could go in and see her. How she looked lying in bed – she looked beautiful and

Simon and Abi playing in our garden in Hull

asleep. It was a bit odd that there was a tube in her nose, but she just looked like Abi asleep.

The environment created some awkwardness – you said it's OK to kiss her – so I did do that. I kissed her on the cheek and I remember the smell, not quite antiseptic, more a clean baby smell. It was funny visiting Abi – although we could talk to her, she couldn't talk back to us.

I didn't know if she was going to wake up; how serious it was; what the problem was. It was odd to visit her and get nothing back from her, especially given the kind of little girl she was. The sadness was not being able to communicate with her. Another memory was when Dad had visited her and he was crying – one of the very few times I saw Dad cry – he was sitting on this very sofa in fact. That was frightening – seeing Dad cry. My memories are all snapshots because it was so long ago."

I suppose it is hard looking back because you can project feelings you have now into the little boy you were then. Do you remember feeling frightened then?

"Yes and a bit confused. I suppose I just didn't know what was going on. I suppose seeing Dad's reaction prompted me to worry more. And it was a severe clinical environment. That wasn't scary so much as alien really. I suppose I might have expected to see her on a ward in a bed with other children around. It was fairly obvious that the situation was pretty serious – and that was frightening. I don't remember having any idea of outcomes."

Did anyone tell you anything, did you ask any questions?

"I don't remember that, either asking or being told things.

I'm sure I had an understanding that she was ill and in the best place she could be. We all used to go as a family to visit the wards Dad worked on in the hospital on Christmas Day – so I knew hospital was a good place to be but I suppose that's at odds with me being confused."

Hospital is a good place to go to get better, but you knew it was serious because you saw Dad crying so perhaps you were confused about whether she would get better or not.

"I think I was too young to understand that there was a chance she wouldn't get better."

It sounds like you understood more than we expected a six year old would be able to understand.

"I understood she was seriously ill, but I wasn't prepared for her dying."

How did you know she had died?

"I feel I can remember that part quite strongly. My memory is that all of us were sitting in a room and in my memory Granny Nel and Granny and Grandpa were there too. And the doctors were attending to Abi, Dad was with them – he came into the room with them. The doctor spoke and as I remember he said he was very sorry to tell us that our sister Abigail had died. I remember it like that because I thought – crazy little thoughts – how odd there are so many people in the room, but he said it was our sister."

Do you think that was a good way to phrase it then?

"Yes, because in one way it showed that the doctor understood the weight of what he was saying to us – what

it meant to us. Seemed like a really kind thing to do – to address we children like that."

It's important to make sure children understand, and it's difficult to tell them about situations like that, particularly when the three of you were different ages and had different levels of understanding. What about the fact that we were all together in that room?

"I was glad of that – we should have been all together then. I've no memory of after that point."

I was with Abi in hospital during that week and Dad went back and forth between there and home. You were at school for the first day at least and came to visit her once or twice. We tried to keep things as normal as we could – that seems crazy looking back, when life was so utterly abnormal and was never going to become normal again as it had been in the past.

What do you remember about the funeral and the celebration meeting we had at home later on?

"I don't remember very much, I remember wondering what a funeral would be like. I had no idea at all. I remember being there – but it's a really vague memory. Sitting and seeing her coffin and I think there were far less people than I expected to be there. But that was because I had no idea what to expect. I don't remember anything that was said. I remember playing with other children upstairs during the meeting at our house and, in a way, a few years later I felt a bit guilty about that. I thought I shouldn't have been playing on a day like that.

I did remember Abi that day though. But then I realised I was only a little boy, what I did that day wouldn't have upset her. Adrian from next door said a few words – 'non-vicary' words; it was nice that he was speaking just as a man. I remember a lot of people being there. There were pictures of Abi around the place stuck on card, which was lovely. And I can remember the mood – it was bitter-sweet, hard to describe – when people are sad about death but they are able to be happy about the life of the person and you know it must be a real effort to try and force yourself and not be sad you've lost them. It seems it would be impossible to achieve that, but just try to do that."

Do you think people were trying to do that on that day?

"I remember you saying that the day was about being thankful for her life, not mourning her death. Making the effort to do that made it a positive occasion – I learnt from that that it is possible to be positive about bereavement. I felt the same thing, in a different way, when Granny Nel died. The memorial meeting we had for Granny was a really lovely day. That reminded me how important it is not to get lost in grief but make sure you remember the person."

I have often wondered about the effect on you, being the youngest child, and moving in and out of that role because of what happened in our family. Have you thought about that and the effect on you?

"Yes, I have – I remember you explaining that when I was about 18 or so. We'd read an article about birth order – I realised what it meant to our family and me in particular and that I hadn't really thought about it before. At the time, when I was a child I thought about Matthew and Cathy doing things together before I came along – fighting like crazy but they did things together too. I thought Abi and I would do some things like that together too at some

point, so I would have a sibling of my own, younger than me. I remember the time when Abi, you and I went to Newcastle together – I saw the photos from that time. The others had a little brother and I had no-one younger than me. I would do whatever Matthew told me and I wanted someone like that too. There were lots of aspects that I looked forward to about having a little sister, but I don't really know what effect it had on me."

**Simon (possibly posing for the camera)
and Abi in Dundee**

Has losing Abi shaped how you view the world, the point of life, what you want from life? Have you thought about that much?

"It's affected me in all those areas – quite deeply. I don't quite understand how or in what way, but I am sure that my view of the world and my place in it has been affected."

So how do you view it? What are you here for?

(Simon was quiet here for a long time; pondering before speaking again.)

"Well, I don't really know what I am here for."

Maybe that is an unfair question – you might be in the process of working it out – being your age now.

"In a way Abi dying has given me the purpose of not dying; of outliving you and Dad."

You have to do that?

"I have to do that, yes. It was unfair that we all lost her in the first place."

Has that thought been in your head a lot over the years?

"Yes, it's been there as a thought rather than a feeling. Because I was so young I accepted it. Life is unfair, many people have had far worse things happen to them, but others have had far better experiences of life."

It sounds like you understood that bit about life being unfair even as a six year old – lots of people much older than that find that concept very difficult to accept or understand.

"I knew you'd, or we'd, lost a baby before Abi – I don't remember anything about that, but I always knew it had happened. Maybe that told me that life was unfair. Abi dying just reinforced it. My grandfather died before I was born – that's unfair but that's just the way it was."

What you said, "My purpose being here is not to die, I'm not going to do that", my guess is that this crossed your mind when you were very low and depressed.

"Yes, it's inevitable, however low I get, I will still be here."

Do you have two voices talking in your head? Does it take a lot of effort to make the low depressed voice listen to the more upbeat voice inside?

"Not really. The low one keeps talking but it can't argue with that reasoning. Abi has died and you don't deserve to lose another child."

Do you ever wonder what she would be like now?

"If I think about it, I tend to romanticise it too much. I've memories of her being alive and well, and it seems to me she can't have been perfect. My memory is of her being sweet and charming and funny – no-one had a bad thing to say about her."

That's true of children, it's easy to fix a memory like that, but she could be a monkey too. A child died and an angelic aura can be created. You might not ever remember the naughty things she did – how she stole things from you, ate your sweets, scribbled on your books.

"I don't remember anything like that, but I seem to remember thinking when she was alive that she never did anything naughty. I didn't do much that was naughty, but I did sometimes. I didn't think she was a goody two shoes though either. Maybe she was just nice to me. As far as what I think her purpose was – I'm a little bit uncomfortable thinking there is someone who directs us

and engineers someone's purpose. But I've often thought, because it seemed so futile when someone so young dies, that it is hard to see any intent. Maybe her purpose was to live, be wonderful and then die. Everyone's purpose is to live and then die, her life just wasn't so long as other people's. Then my memory is so coloured by the fact that she died. Easy to think that's all she did – arrived and then died. I'm sure that's not true, she did plenty of stuff. But I think the fact of her dying taught me that everyone dies."

A hard lesson to learn when you are just six years old – that all that happens is that we are born, we live our life for however long that is and then we die.

"Yes and a sad one. I've been aware of that since then, maybe before too. I don't know how valuable a lesson it's been."

We never had any pets when you were young. Often parents give their children pets so they can learn about caring for something other than themselves, and about mortality and death. So as far as teaching you about mortality – you had a much bigger lesson. What Abi did have was a lot of little friends. So did you, there were loads of people you were close to at school. Have you any memories of that time and going back to school after she had died?

"No, even though I still know some of those friends now and are good friends with them. I don't remember the teachers saying anything. I did leave class a couple of times to cry and teachers were sympathetic. There was no choice for me – if I felt like bursting into tears I just went out of class."

As you moved to a new school and then later on to college and then university, meeting new people who ask about you and your family, what has that been like for you? What do you say about your brothers and sisters?

"At the new school I went to when I was 11, I was drifting between different groups, trying out different friendships. I told a boy I thought was a friend about Abi and he didn't believe me. I didn't try to convince him because it seemed a ridiculous thing to lie about. Ever since then I've been reluctant to tell people unless I know them well. Basically I don't unless it comes up or I am a good friend with them. Even then I would have to wait for it to come up naturally. There is a guy at work – we've been friends for a year – I told him what I was doing tonight, because there was no reason not to tell him. I said it was 20 years ago, but he was still cagey. It can be awkward to tell people."

What about girlfriends, have you found a way to talk to them?

"I've only had two girlfriends but that is easier in a way because with friends you just talk about whatever, with girls you're trying to get to know each other much more deeply, so it's much more natural."

So what about other friends, men?

"I've not that many friends, but there are one or two women friends I've known since I was very young and before Abi died. I can't think of that many people I've volunteered the information to. I told a flatmate when I didn't know him very well, it was soon after I moved into his house and we were looking at photos. It's a nice friendship to be able to do that. Whenever I talk about it I am vulnerable."

Do you worry you might get upset?

"I'm not anxious about it, but I know I might, or that I might start off thinking..."

That was a powerful experience – the boy at school who didn't believe you. Why would you make up something like that?

"Adults aren't that stupid, but it made me aware that I may not get the reaction I expect or it's something very personal to the family, a deep part of all of us, and to share with someone else requires something different."

You're vulnerable, you don't know what the response might be, it can be a conversation killer and you have to manage the situation. It can be quite a deterrent to tell anyone, can't it? Have any of your friends had bereavements in their lives?

"One or two people I have known over the years have been bereaved, and all I can say is I think it has helped me to understand what they are going through. In a way it made me grateful for having suffered a bereavement – my friends knew about that and I could help."

It strikes me that you did talk about Abi when you were little, but not very much. I don't think I ever pushed you; we just did the best we could at the time. I guess you thought about her a lot, so do you wish Dad and I had made more opportunities for you to talk about her, or that you could talk to anyone else like grandparents?

"I think I could have done if I had wanted to. I remember I used to come downstairs after I had gone to bed because I was upset because she had died. I remember I did that a

fair bit; it almost became a habit. I don't know – I thought back about that, and that there you and Dad were in your grief and a little boy came downstairs crying – there was no choice for you but to deal with him whether you wanted to or not. I have no memories of how you coped at the time. You must have been strong for us."

Dad and I were being as strong as we could be. I think that when you are feeling very raw with grief, it is actually very comforting to have a little boy come down and want a cuddle. I think it probably did me good. The part I worry about is a bit late now, that if I had felt stronger I could have helped you to talk more if that would have helped you. You may not know the answer to that anyway. We did our best, but some things may have been inappropriate. Some things we did were completely mad when I remember.

Was there anything that helped, like books, poetry, music?

"Certain unexpected songs from early to mid-80s – could be anything – they just touch a nerve. I don't know if I'm making this up but a year or so after she died, I began to play the French horn, and I think there is some kind of link with Abi. I never played the horn while she was alive. I made that connection: about the fact I had taken it up not long after she died. Maybe I threw myself into it – perhaps it gave me some solace? A few weeks ago playing the guitar I realised that I can lose myself in the playing and the music. Maybe it was a comfort that I found for myself. It separates me from my emotions – I have to concentrate on making the sounds."

Do you have any idea when things started to get easier?

"It's difficult to know really. I remember the period of grief, and after that I seemed to accept it and be OK. I do remember a time when I was out with some friends (I was about 15) – I'd had a bit to drink. I didn't get upset in those days, but I got upset then and it was the first time I had thought about her and been upset for a long time. It triggered me to think about her more and about how her loss was affecting me. I felt it was easy to hang my problems on her death and the past. Maybe that's the reason, not the excuse."

Did you ever wonder how Matthew and Cathy were coping with it?

"I assumed that Cathy was coping much worse than me or Matthew – because I knew she had a special bond with Abi, being both girls."

You knew that?

"It felt like I knew that. Cathy wasn't an enemy of me or Matthew, but she could enjoy a relationship with Abi because they were girls, and I knew she liked having a sister. Cathy did some pictures once, when Abi was alive and well – of what Abi would look like when she was older."

I am amazed, again, by your memory. Do you think losing Abi accentuated the differences between the three of you?

"A little bit, yes. Matthew and I felt it, but Cathy's loss was greater – her only sister. That might not be true. Perhaps we all five dealt with our grief on our own. When we left 126 and moved house, I walked to school with Cathy that day. She was crying and I didn't really talk to her."

Did you feel she was embarrassing to be with? That was in 1987 so you would be nine.

"No, not that, I remember her crying and thinking I don't really want to ask her about this, it may just be about leaving the house, I assumed it was that, and also Abi."

What about you at that time? Was it a relief to move house?

"I don't remember any feelings about that. In a way I had accepted she had gone. I had the memories still; the different house wouldn't change that. I looked forward to the move, it was all exciting."

Was there anything you would have liked us to have done but we didn't, perhaps mark her birthday in some way? We never did that, sometimes we would mention it, but we never made a point of talking about her.

"That brings up a few things. I remember us being on holiday in France, we were all together in the big tent and when you or Dad, I can't remember who, brought up her name everyone shut up and stopped talking. Dad said, 'look we can't get all sad every time we mention her; we can't not talk about her'. I remember seeing the sense in that. She was a part of the family. From that I knew you and Dad, with a more mature attitude, were the directors of how we should be. You challenged us to remember her, she was very important.

And there was another time, closer to when she died. I think you said we had to try and remember who she was. I must have taken that on to remember it. It was much more important to remember that, rather than the fact she had died. I don't think there's anything you should have

139

done that you didn't. I remember her birthday, I always do, and how old she would have been. I spoke to Cathy once on Abi's birthday. Cathy was having a drink for her – but it's pointless, because she isn't here and we don't know what she would have done.

I do think about Abi a lot, but I try not to. I don't want to let myself think about what would she have been like, what she would have been doing and so on."

So you would push those thoughts away?

"I used to when I was younger. One last night of the holidays I realised she would have been old enough to go to Senior School and she would have probably been going with me. I had an imaginary conversation with her – I found it very comforting to do that. Told her what it would be like and so on."

Have you ever felt, at the time, or later, her presence with you?

"I don't know – I see her in places. Little girls: I think about having my own children, and maybe seeing Abi in a daughter. I'm slightly frightened of that – not of losing a child – but I wonder if there's a temptation to think she could live the life Abi would have lived."

It's not likely you would do that, because you've been aware of that from being much younger.

"My feelings could be about my long-dead sister, rather than my daughter, but I think the daughter would override all those feelings. So no, I'm not that worried."

I have wondered if the loss of Abi meant you weren't going to settle down and have children, but I don't want to put pressure on you. You sound as if you have made your own sense of what happened; it sounds like you got your own understanding about what it meant losing her. If and when you have children, I think you'll find it will be a really joyful experience and you'll be a fantastic father.

Is there anything you want to know about or ask me about?

"I feel uncomfortable about wanting to know, but I haven't ever really been sure of what was wrong with her."

He wanted to know the medical history of what happened, even though he thought it wasn't that important. Our conversation came to a close after we spent some time talking about it and me telling him as much as I could. I hope that I was able to fill in some of the gaps for him. I think he will gain more once he has read this, and he has contributed so much to the whole picture.

Simon had plenty of reflections later on and more questions about what had happened. He appears much more down-to-earth and at ease than Matthew is when the two of them talk about Abi and the past. Simon had helpful ideas about what would be useful in this book too.

I found some of our conversation hard to hear, particularly the part about his determination to make sure Paddy and I didn't have to go through losing another child. For whatever reason, Simon has found it difficult to find his place in the world, what he wants to do at work and so on. How much this has been influenced by Abi's death, I will never know. To some extent, this is now changing.

But I think the whole process of working out what he wants out of life has been a very hard one for him.

I also thought later about how, even though he was only six, his memory and the way he described the events was almost stronger than the others. I think the very fact of his young age contributed to that. His description of the doctors coming to tell us that Abi had died conveyed the weight of the experience. It has stayed with him more than the others and it conjured up for me a real picture of the group of us, sitting isolated in our despair and grief, knowing what was coming and willing it not to be true.

The doctor's words took away any form of disbelief – this is how it is and you are going to have to deal with it. He delivered such a stark message – I remember thinking how callous he sounded, but in fact I think it was the best way because it took away any possibility of hope or that they might have made a mistake. The doctors knew the precise facts of the situation, had come to their conclusions and there was no room for any questions or doubt. It has taken me a long time to reach that understanding when I remember the experience. Simon's memory of that and the fact that the way in which we were told actively helped him to understand has helped me immeasurably.

It was a real comfort for me to learn that it had really helped Simon to feel important, so that he understood what had happened. I can imagine he could have had very different feelings if a different approach had been made. I remembered that I had felt very resentful towards that surgeon for a long time for the manner of his talking to us, and once I realised Simon's point of view, it helped to free that up.

I had another realisation about a further aspect of the grief process, in that the loss of potential experiences for the future is another kind of bereavement. Simon missed out on times which would have been very special and particular to Abi and him, had she lived. The older two children had gone away to stay with grandparents on their own, as well as to stay with cousins and friends' families. Simon missed out on this. I know I wanted to keep him close to me and didn't want him to grow up too fast. I did exactly the same thing previously when my baby died in 1980.

Our conversation was another example of one of the children having an upsetting experience that I didn't know about. Thinking about it now, I feel so sad that I didn't know about those times, that my children protected me from some of the grief and hard times they were going through. I am, of course, unsure whether their teachers knew about these occasions, but if so, they didn't let me know. Perhaps if I had known I could have had a conversation with my children to help them work out how to handle situations such as these.

Until we spoke, I had never thought about Simon using music as a form of escapism and way of switching off from the world. He is the most musical of the three of the children, although all of them enjoy music and have wide tastes. I've always viewed the French horn as the most difficult instrument in the world. He was going to play the trumpet, like Matthew, but a friend of his got the last trumpet at school. So he took that big challenge on – then he realised that music gave him comfort, and a space in which he didn't have to think. He is very understated about his talents, he composes his own music and I think he is the complete opposite of 'blowing your own trumpet'.

I imagine sport can have a similar effect too, losing oneself in the moment of concentrating on what is happening. Both sport and music also give the experience of being part of a team or an orchestra and the positive effects of those groups.

Given the time lapse between our first conversation and now, lots has happened in his life. He is now married and settled with Claire, although he still seems to me to be searching for his fulfilment at work. When he writes music and plays that with his friends, then he seems to be fulfilled. Perhaps it will give him his creative outlet and satisfy him that way, and eventually he will find the path he wants through work.

Eight

Rosalind

Rosalind is my father's sister, and she has always been present in my life as a source of love and support. She is a very generous, quiet and private woman and I have always seen her as having a strong faith, whatever that might mean. To me, I have always felt that she had an easy understanding of what God meant to her. I have seen her being a true Christian, particularly in the way she helps others less fortunate than herself, but she never rams God or her faith down anyone's throat. It has seemed as if her relationship with her church has got stronger as she has got older; it plays a central role in her life and much of her social life appears to revolve around her church. She talks enthusiastically about how her church is full of young people and how it caters for them, to ensure that their church has a vibrant future.

I have never talked to her about my feelings about anything that could be described as 'deep' which made me wonder how this conversation would be. I realised a few years ago how important a figure she was in my life when she had a malignant melanoma removed from her leg. I felt a real need then to contact her and make sure she was all right. The question about asking her whether she was willing to talk to me was removed from me by Alison, my mother, telling her what I was doing and that I would be contacting her. I thought she was a bit nervous about it, and she said she wasn't sure what she could remember, so was unsure what help she could be.

I know that she is a good listener, and that she has hidden depths; I am sure there are things she does which I'm not aware of. This also reminded me that she has visited patients in hospital, where she is a voluntary visitor on the chaplaincy team. She speaks to patients on a ward, regardless of their faith, introducing herself as from the chaplaincy, but having a general conversation and hopefully, "bringing some comfort or cheer to them". Very occasionally she is asked to pray with them.

Do you remember much about what happened at the time?

"I can't remember a lot really, Alison phoned me at the beginning of the week, probably on the Wednesday, to tell me Abi was very ill. She was going down to Hull to help you. All I can remember is that I went into my bedroom and shut the door and knelt down and really, really prayed. I don't usually pray although I might talk to God in the morning."

I know you have a very strong faith.

"I wouldn't say that..."

My perception is that your faith is important and has a real place in your life. You are the only person who had that in the family, so that was one reason why I was so interested to find out more about that.

"I can remember feeling very agitated, I don't know how long I prayed. I was really pleading with God for Abi to get better. Then I felt at peace. I felt it would be all right, then it wasn't all right and then we have to come to terms with that."

How do you do that?

"Well I'm sure God doesn't want people to die: He allows it."

If people have been here long enough? Or been on the earth to do what they need?

"Difficult to understand why children should die, there must be some reason why God should allow it."

You haven't found it?

"No, there are lots of things we won't know why in this life – like the tsunami, why did God allow that to happen? I believe He is still sovereign. The only way I could come to terms with it, for some reason. Look what you've done since Abi died and how you've counselled people and all this work talking to us all – you might not have done this if Abi hadn't died."

No, nor be the woman I am today without Abi dying – it's one of the ways I can get something positive from it.

"I believe in God and He has a plan and all things work together for good."

Perhaps that's the kind of thing you can't say at the time.

"No, it takes a while to work through this and think why, why should this happen. Then you can see a greater good coming out."

When you said you prayed and that had helped – but then it didn't work, Abi didn't get better. How did you feel when Abi died, do you remember that?

"I felt kind of let down, or wondered why, why God, why have you done this? It takes a while to work through it."

Did you do that on your own or talk to someone at the church?

"Yes, at church. I was doing the flowers – I can remember standing by the flower stand in church on the Sunday and someone came up and asked if I was all right. I told her about it but she didn't really help. Can't remember what she said, but it was no help although she's the sort of person who would be a help normally. I just worked through it on my own."

I have been thinking about when Bert[16] died, that must have hit you really hard as well.

"Well it's interesting, that lady I just mentioned who I told about what happened to Abi, when Bert died she phoned the minister and he came to see me. So she was a help. Not at the time when Abi died, but she must have felt I needed help when Bert died. The minister was different when Abi died and he was no help at all. The last minister was there for seven years, I was on the appointments committee, and he was the right man for the church and for me. A shame he only stayed seven years.

I remember that one evening I went to see Anthony, he was alone and I remember how upset he was. I didn't think I would be any help to him, I wanted to, but it's so difficult to know what to say. Maybe just being there is enough. He said how helpful Dr Kelleher, one of his partners, had been. I do remember that."

---

[16]   Bert was a friend of hers for many years and was a very important person in her life.

148

This is interesting: one person remembers one thing and someone else doesn't and it all comes together to make a bigger picture. Either I forgot things, or I didn't know. This all helps me to flesh it out and understand what other people were going through.

We arranged the funeral just for our immediate family, how did you feel about that? In a way, we excluded you but it wasn't deliberately because we weren't thinking straight.

"That was OK, it was what you wanted."

You came to the celebration meeting at our house.

"That was just a week after. I remember you cleaning your shoes, saying you had to clean your shoes."

I'd forgotten about that and it feels such unusual behaviour for me. I suppose it was like me doing something atypical, me coping and doing something practical without having to talk to people because I couldn't talk, it was so difficult for me.

"I remember Annie being there, and I remember coming away and talking to you at the door. I felt I just didn't know what to say that could be of any comfort."

What was it like? You were upset; you loved both me and Abi. It's like you were watching from a distance, how we were, how I was with my parents, how they were when I wasn't there and you coming to terms and understanding too. Is there anything which strikes you about that?

"I do remember how upset Alison was for a long, long time."

Did she ever talk to you much?

"Yes, she did. We didn't sit down and have a long conversation; she was often in tears. Perhaps Anthony was getting a bit impatient with her, because she would go on and on, and he would get a bit irritable. His way was to say we can't do anything about it, it's happened. Just the impression I got. Obviously he was very upset too, and he copes in a more inward, quieter way."

(I noticed that when she referred to how my parents coped together she was careful about what she was saying, as if she wasn't sure about it and uncertain of her assessment of how they were managing.)

Did you carry on praying after she died?

"Praying for Abi? Whoever – everyone. I prayed for you and Paddy."

Thank you.

"But I knew that she would be all right, wherever she was. I don't quite know what happens to children; I can't think God wouldn't let them into heaven just because they haven't said I believe in you. There must be somewhere for children..."

What happens to adults after they die?

"I think Jesus came – God is the God of love and of justice and mercy and you can't have any sin in His presence. That's why Jesus came to die in our place so we can go and be with God and repent of our sins. We have to do that in our lifetime on earth. Children haven't had the opportunity to do that."

One thing I've wondered about is whether books, music, poetry were any help or not helpful?

"There is a chorus we sing at church sometimes: 'He gives and takes away but my heart will continue to bless you Lord, even though you give and take away, blessed be the name of the Lord'."

That has helped? As a kind of reminder?

"Yes, yes it has. Lots of things at church have helped because God loves us so much and He doesn't want bad things to happen but they do and He helps us through."

It doesn't sound as though your faith was rocked by Abi dying?

"No, but I know some people can be like that."

Did it go the other way; did it strengthen your faith?

"I don't know really. When my father died I was very upset for a long time and I couldn't talk about him. That was 1957, when I was 28 and I couldn't talk to your grandma at all."

Did she talk to you? You came back to live with her after a year. Did you do that on purpose to come and live with her?

"Yes, that worked out well. You see I think God is planning our lives and we don't see it at the time. So looking back, God has been guiding my life."

Things work together and slot in.

"I loved working in the lab at the Royal Victoria Infirmary after I came back to Newcastle to live with your grandma."

It was a big thing, to go away from home for four years and then come back and live with your mother. That's what Cathy is doing now! (Cathy was living with us in between completing her MA in Oxford and beginning her journalism course, so Paddy, she and I were finding out what it was like to live together again after a gap of 12 years or so.)

"In those days being upset meant you didn't talk to anyone. I knew at the time that my father was happy, I could see him and he was laughing. He had a lovely laugh, so even though I was sad, I knew he was all right."

Is that like you imagining him or could you see him?

"No, it was only in my mind, I've never had any experiences like that.

When your grandma died it was very different because she had been ill, and I didn't want her to suffer any more. She did suffer then. Things like pain control are so much better these days."

Maybe you grieved for her on your own, rather than talking to anyone?

"Yes, but my brothers, Anthony and Philip, were both helpful, writing letters and so on. In actual fact they did most of the arrangements, I didn't have to do anything like that."

Is this OK, looking back and talking about that kind of thing?

"Yes, I can talk now."

You said about grieving in private and that is what you do. Here am I asking you questions I've never asked you before or to remember things we've never talked about, I don't want to push you somewhere you don't want to go.

"I don't mind at all. Quite often when I have Anthony and Alison over for a meal we talk about our parents."

Maybe it's different remembering things that happened, events and so on, compared with talking about feelings and how you were when either one of your parents died. I'm asking you to talk about something that you clearly decided when you were much younger that you weren't going to talk about to anyone in the family.

"I couldn't, I knew I would break down and be in tears so I shut it away. I don't like crying in front of people. I think it is a culture in this country – the British stiff upper lip; no, I don't like it. We had an Egyptian chap at my church, he was hoping for a liver transplant, but he died and his wife came over. I'm not sure whether she couldn't get a visa, but his daughter was here with him. His wife came for his funeral and she was wailing and crying out his name. We just don't do that, but it is their culture. A lot of things that affect you also affect the way other people may think about you.

I remember that you didn't want to leave the house and didn't want the stairs to be re-painted because of her little fingermarks up the stairs. It must have been hard for you, but things get better with time. Do you look back and see the landmarks when things were getting better?"

Well, I think we stayed in Hull too long and we should have moved away earlier. When we moved from Hull to Little Weighton it was a halfway house really and not far enough away. Looking back, I don't know, if someone said move away, I wouldn't have said, "No, you don't know what you're talking about", because I was too polite. But if we had been able to listen to a suggestion it might actually have helped us to move on. With everything we just did what we thought was best at the time. All kinds of things, talking to the children, making choices with information we had at the time and trying to do our best. It might have been more helpful to have moved further away, but then where we lived was so convenient for school and work, and we had lots of friends around us. We were too vulnerable to take that step.

Anything you have observed about the way I have coped with this, things you might have liked to say to me over the years, but didn't? Or about how the children have been?

"I know Matthew still gets very upset and he can't talk about Abi. I know you have dealt with it, by doing this counselling. I don't know if you don't work yourself too hard but perhaps that is your way of coping with it. I think it's good, to have your work and that outlet."

I suppose I've wondered over the years, thinking about people in the family who are a part of our lives, if there were things they wanted to say but we put the shutters up and whether we were unapproachable just because we were hurting too much. Were there words of advice you might have had, that kind of thing?

"Well in a way I don't think you can advise people. You want to help but you don't know the right way to help, and in a sense everyone has to work it out for themselves."

I think that too – that you need to work it out for yourself. It has occurred to me to wonder, though, whether people saw us and felt like saying why don't you do whatever? What might have stopped them from saying things?

"I think the way you have dealt with it really, and thrown yourself into what you are doing and helping other people come to terms with bereavement. Did I ever write to you at the time?"

You would have done.

"I might not have done if I didn't know what on earth to say."

I'll have to look back through my things. I will look and let you know.

"I wouldn't know what to say. There aren't the right words to say to anyone. A bit of me thinks it's better not to say anything rather than the wrong thing."

One or two friends who were Roman Catholic asked for a mass to be said. I found that very hard and at the time it felt like an intrusion into our grief. It took me quite a long time to realise that it's no different from someone praying or sitting and thinking and sending love towards us. At the time, I was angry about it. I never told them. Looking back that feels unfair because all they were doing was their best and I guess it helped them too.

"Just like a service, praying. Dr Kelleher who helped Anthony, he is a Catholic."

One question I've been asking is something the children find difficult. When people ask about the numbers of brothers and sisters they have, they find it very difficult to know how to answer. It brings up so many questions and sometimes can be a real conversation killer. Does it ever arise for you when people ask you about your family? How do you answer those kinds of questions?

"Well, if anyone has asked, I would say that you had four children and one had died. I would never say you only had three children. But you've had more than four pregnancies?"

Eight.

"Eight!! I thought it was seven."

I have had miscarriages and the last one was in 1994. And I found it incredibly stressful having GIFT.

"That's astonishing and I didn't know what had happened in 1994. Did you have a funeral for the stillborn baby? No, but you should have done."

That's you giving advice! I don't put any blame on anyone, but I don't know what happened about making that decision because I was ill. Now I know that we should have had a funeral for her. But Paddy being Paddy, he would have said to the hospital, "Just take care of everything, so that I can take care of my wife", but that really wasn't a good idea. The thinking has changed now and there are all sorts of memories such as keeping locks of hair, hand-prints, photos. We have nothing at all, which is really sad.

What do you think of me doing this?

"It's a really good idea, Christine. I know when children go through a traumatic experience, they get them to do drawings and this is the same sort of thing. I don't know if they do with adults, but I think it's good to get all your thoughts clarified, and maybe ask yourself questions: was this right; should we have done this. Just to get things sorted out in your mind. It's a lot of work; good, but a lot of work."

Anything else which comes to mind?

"I'll probably go on thinking about it after you've gone."

You do a lot of hospital visiting so you must be a good listener.

"Listening and letting the silence be; there are people who don't listen at all. I am interested in people. I love people and everyone has a story and everyone is different. I don't go preaching at the hospital; I listen and I don't joke with them, I try and have a nice smile for them. If I can be of any help, that's what I want to do."

I'm sure that's what people want, someone with a nice smile to come to the bed.

"Could Simon remember much?"

Far more than I expected, but of course he has a photographic recall. When he was little if he'd seen a film or read a book, he would describe the whole story to us. He had quite a lot of memories which were different from Cathy so that was quite a surprise. Matthew has already said that he can't remember anything. I don't necessarily think that's true.

I haven't talked to Matthew yet but I know that it will be important for him to talk about it. Otherwise when he has children he could find it very difficult because he hasn't understood his feelings about children and his fears about them perhaps dying.

We ended our conversation there and I said I would type it up and send it to her, so she could check what she had said and see if there was anything to change or add.

When she later read through the transcript of our conversation, she told me that she wouldn't describe herself as a 'great pray-er' – especially not in public - because she is too self-conscious, but she usually has a time in the morning before she gets up when she talks to God and she has certain topics to pray for. She was very thoughtful and reflective before answering my questions and later remembered that a friend had given her a book of poetry which had included a poem about pain which she found useful.

I found this conversation with Rosalind very helpful. I enjoyed the time with her because we were talking in a way that I don't think we ever had done before. One aspect was finding out about her feelings and the experience of losing her parents (my grandparents). Our meeting was yet another example to me of her generosity of heart. It was only as we talked that I wondered if she had felt excluded from Abi's funeral, but through our conversation it seemed that she had never thought that.

I have wondered over the time since our conversation whether it resulted in a shift in our relationship. She has recently talked about the special bond she feels between us. I certainly feel closer to her and think I know more about her.

Nine

Anthony

My parents were and are a very important part of my life therefore I have chosen to have their interviews as the concluding ones. There is a special bond between mother and daughter, and the connection between me and my mother and my experience of being Abi's mother feels important and unique so it feels right to have my mother's conversation with me at the end.

They have always been supportive, helping me develop and work out what I wanted to do as a teenager, encouraging me to find a career for myself when I decided university wasn't to be my next step. I sought their advice at many stages in my life and they were among the first people I shared happy or exciting experiences with, as well as concerns or anxieties.

One strong message when I was growing up was that if there are problems, you face them and just get on with life – practical ways of coping were the way to do it. Yet there is an anomaly here – I saw how my parents coped with problems in a practical way, but also how my mother in particular would worry about things and want to talk about them over and over. I saw that as not having a real purpose; that it was just the act of talking that she wanted, rather than finding some kind of rationale or resolution to whatever it was that was troubling her. So does that mean that I thought talking was pointless? Not that, but more that I needed to find the right person for me to talk to.

My closeness to them was the very thing that got in the way. I knew without being told that one of the hardest things for them was not knowing how to help me when I was hurting so much. They could also see how much agony I was in, and that must have left them feeling very helpless. The loss of their granddaughter was compounded by my anguish and sorrow, Paddy's devastation and their other grandchildren who were desolate without their little sister. They felt helpless, and perhaps really helpless for the first time in their lives. It is only through this process that I have really understood more about their feelings and the depth to which they were suffering themselves.

Inklings of this must have been swirling around in my mind and as the years passed I often wanted to find a way to talk about how I felt and find out more about what it was like for them. I think this became more prominent in my mind as I approached the age at which I might become a grandparent myself! Added to that was the fact that I knew they weren't going to be around forever. They held feelings, knowledge, understandings and emotions about that time that would disappear when they died unless I found a way to unlock the barrier between us. I guessed it would be a challenging thing to ask them to talk to me about that time, but of course as soon as I asked them they were unequivocal about agreeing to it. I later discovered that my father was not so sure about the wisdom of it, but my mother was 100% supportive.

I realised that just the fact of me asking them for their help, and then talking about why I wanted to do this, was beginning to unlock things just a little. They are always so conscious of not wanting me 'to do too much' or take on too much work and yet they also know even as they mention those kinds of thoughts that I don't welcome that kind of intrusion!   I was aware as I listened to them as we talked, and then played back the recording, that there may still be things they have kept to themselves for fear of hurting me more – as if they could.

It felt more challenging to talk to my father than my mother. Partly I think this is because he is more reticent about his feelings than she is and I was aware that over the years, he seemed to be unhappy that she still wanted to talk about Abi. Maybe I had picked up that he thought she should have 'moved on'. The other aspect was that I felt that he thought this was perhaps a risky thing to do, that I could be opening up old wounds again.

He began by saying how he remembered Simon talking after Abi had died about her moneybox and saying, "We can divide it out now between us".

"How old was he?"

He was about six.

"If Simon was six, Cathy eight or thereabouts, that's really too young to feel the loss in emotional terms."

I think given what Cathy and Simon have remembered, it shows that they did feel the loss, despite their age. Perhaps they didn't understand what it really meant?

"Matthew being the eldest could feel in detail."

Did he ever talk to you about it?

"No, no."

My impression is they haven't talked to you at all.

"No, but this applies to you and Paddy as well as the children. It's clear as soon as her name is mentioned; it's not exactly like the shutters come down, but a feeling that this is such a distressing time in everyone's life that we are all still grieving and will go on grieving. I feel, at any rate, that grief has to be borne personally and privately and it is not a topic for dinner table conversation. It will always be like that."

(He said that last sentence very precisely and clearly, and it felt a little like a gentle warning – don't push me too far.)

It sounds like our reaction to Abi's death didn't surprise you, but of course you've been involved with so many people over the years in your work as a General Practitioner.

"A number of people over the years. Our experience then wasn't atypical."

Even so, it doesn't make it easier when you are the person it has happened to.

"That's true. So many people, my patients and their relatives and friends, and it never ceases to amaze me how enormous the differences are."

In what kinds of ways?

"Well, there is the example of someone we knew who died recently where the family were sitting round the bed drinking gin and tonics. I cannot imagine doing that and I've never known anyone else do that sort of thing."

So do you wish we had been able to talk about Abi more, and what it's been like for us?

"Yes I think so, indeed."

Did the lead need to come from Paddy and me?

"I don't think I can agree with that exactly – as a doctor one becomes really quite tolerant of the different ways people behave. You just have to accept that people react differently. Knowing Paddy as I do, I wouldn't really expect him to. Paddy and I can talk about medical matters dispassionately, but we couldn't do that with something so intimate as a child's illness. A lot goes through my mind in connection with her illness before the death.

Anger to begin with – one goes through all the stages of bereavement. At the time I felt it very difficult to understand how it could have happened in a medical household."

Angry with us, or Paddy in particular?

"Angry with Paddy? Yes, I think so to some degree, and with the hospital situation. It was quite clear that things could have been managed differently. I feel that now after all these years; it's no good dwelling on that because it can't be changed."

How did you deal with that? I wouldn't have known and would never have guessed you were angry with us. I would have imagined your anger, but not guessed angry with us or me.

"Not angry with you at all, I felt you were going through a time of severe anguish – it's no good blaming someone who is suffering so intensely. I don't think I have ever seen anyone suffering as much as you did."

(I could really hear the anguish in his voice.)

"Abi wasn't in your arms when I arrived, she was on a support system, so you could throw your arms round me and say you were so sorry. It was quite clear it was absolute agony as far as you were concerned – no-one could blame someone suffering that agony. If I'm honest, I blame Paddy more than anyone, but also the hospital staff, from the medical consultant downwards. I never met the consultant, or nursing staff – they were just a blur in the background. My feelings were focussed on you and Abi."

Did you ever talk to anyone?

"I talked to Alison at great length. If she has strong feelings or worries about something, we worry it to death and go over and over it again and again – talk about a 'dog with a bone'! I don't think it's productive, rather, I think it makes it worse."

What about at work? Did you talk to any of the partners?

"I must have mentioned it. I can vaguely recollect enormous sympathy. I'm very fortunate that I've worked in a practice where we were all good friends, all sympathetic; Jim and Rick and David in particular."

We asked you to read something from The Prophet at the celebration meeting we had. The whole thing was a blur for me.

"I can't remember. I can only remember the sun shining. But the funeral was absolutely ghastly, there were so few of us there. Nimrod Variation was played, which I don't really like hearing again. Of all the variations it's the one I like least, even before that day. I remember Paddy being

very abrupt; it was all carried through very quickly, and it didn't appear to be personal, more like going through the motions. I've had a lot of experience of funerals since then, including one or two patients' children's funerals. Funerals do vary – some are very happy occasions – but I can't imagine anything less happy than that.

I don't believe in this business of someone being at rest and it's OK. As far as I'm concerned the body has gone – absolutely. I'm not really one for going to graveyards, unlike Alison."

So where do you get your comfort from, if indeed you do? What did this experience do to your faith?

"The comfort I feel now is that she was a lovely little girl. I remember you coming along the platform at the Central

**Me, my father, Simon and Abi at about the
time he refers to**

Station and she was shy and didn't want to leave you and run to us. Another memory I have is of taking her up to get a Sunday paper – walking along the road. Other people had clearly noticed us and seen us and commented, 'Isn't that lovely'. That is a very clear memory.

And at Westbourne Avenue – she must have been about two – you saying that if something is missing or I can't remember where it is Abi will know. Little children haven't got too much to think about; the world situation doesn't bother them, but where the chocolate biscuits are kept is important to them! As I get older, some memories become clearer."

Must be nice memories to have.

"That's the only way in which we matter to generations that follow, having recollections like that; it's the only influence that remains."

So we need to keep on talking about them. Any idea when or how things started to get or feel a bit easier?

"I'm trying to think – it's an interesting question. It has its ups and downs."

Was there anything which made it worse?

"The downside was visiting you all in Hull. We didn't go that often, but it always rekindled a grief. It was the house really, rather than driving past the hospital, and I can understand why you wanted to move. Though moving doesn't really help. It's the unspoken – there is someone missing."

Thinking about significant birthdays and so on...

"That's right. I've got it in my diary every year – I write it down."

(He got up to make sure he could show me.)

Do you write down her birthday or the day she died?

"Her birthday. I write that in every year – Abigail, 10th December 1981. I have the ages of other people written down on their birthdays – obsessional is my middle name!"

Did it make it easier once we moved house?

"No, I don't think it did, it's not something that Alison and I mentioned. We didn't say, 'Oh dear, poor little Abi', we just remember Abigail. It was just a feeling without being able to say anything more about it. Going back to Hull did rekindle memories – will go on doing so to the end of time."

I imagine it won't go away but it changes over time. What's it like now we are living in York?

"It is much less intense – this is a move forward and so much else has been happening. There is only room in your mind for a limited number of things. We think about all the family and their individual concerns about their work, their lives and so on. All these sort of things, they don't exactly crowd out feelings about Abigail, that's not true, but there is so much happening. There's a limit to how many things you can become involved with."

Was there anything that helped – books, poetry, music?

"I don't know – I've been involved with funerals for some time – I keep all the order of services and quite a number of books kept over the years.

With music – I now hate the Elgar and Nimrod Variation but I don't associate music with Abigail. I associate music with other feelings – including my father's death and the hymns they had at the funeral then. Watching 'Songs of Praise', which I do most Sundays, brings tears to one's eyes sometimes. Music has always made me feel emotional."

It brings back memories of the past?

"Even happy things – like carols at Christmas – can still be emotional."

Who do you think is the person who's helped you most – if there is anyone?

"I don't really know, I can't answer that. Maybe it is just a personal process – it's just me who helps me. Yes, I do feel that. Grief is something private and has to be borne personally. Have to find your own way through it. While on the same theme – you can shout me down or laugh as you wish – but I'm not a great believer in counselling."

It sounds like you believe you have to get through this on your own, and also that you have no wish it was different, or wish you had the opportunity to share more. Any regrets or thoughts about the process of how it has been?

"No, it could have been different but I don't honestly feel... I just accept the way things are. I'm not really a great one for regrets. I really feel life has been very good; I've

been most fortunate in my forebears and in my present family situation and the way things are developing with the family. Things could have been different. And in my career in medicine, at various stages of my life, I have been very fortunate."

Anything you would have liked to have done, but didn't? Perhaps talking about her to certain people, mark her birthday or the day she died?

"I don't know really. There has to come a time when one doesn't have the memorial services, Armistice Day, remembrances of that kind and I'm not really one for family remembrances – of that sort. Birthdays and Christmas are one thing but they are cheerful occasions."

What about meeting new people – when they ask you questions regarding grandchildren, how do you respond?

"Just as Alison does – it happens frequently. We do tell people and we go on to say, 'You can imagine how distressing that was'. People accept that. We tend to meet more people now than we did then. Alison might be different in what she says when she meets new people on her own.

We don't go into things deeply unless someone is very interested. Some concerned people wanted to know the details. However, most people are not concerned but they like to gossip; to know the facts and to build up a picture of someone. They don't want to suffer it with you."

A lot of people said at the time or afterwards what a strong impression she had made on them and it's something I have thought about, the amount of influence she seemed to have.

"Yes, we felt that she was different from the others. A fun person; she had obviously got a strong personality even at that age, just before she was three. She would have been a source of great joy. I used to come across quite a lot of students in practice and boys and girls of 18 or 20 are quite fascinating, because the world is at their feet. You see them making their own mark, making mistakes, doing things they shouldn't be doing and it's quite stimulating. I still find that.

I like young people. I can't cope with it as much physically, but I like the grandchildren in New Zealand, they are great fun, even though they are sometimes difficult. Sam was quite difficult as a teenager; Richard was too – but they are totally different now. Lovely to see the way they blossom. The sort of feelings I remember having about Abi were that she had something special about her, but I didn't see that much of her. She was good fun and a little mischief."

You did keep your grief hidden in the way you described and Mum's was more on the surface. I wondered what that was like for you. It affected her so deeply, what did it do to your relationship?

"It brought us together – very definitely, one or two other things have done that too. Like the two occasions when she went off to New Zealand by herself, I remember saying never again, not a good thing for us to be apart but we realised how close we were. There is no doubt that anxieties bring you together, we do talk about problems but perhaps not as much as we ought to. I am unbearable at times when I have something I either can't or don't want to talk about. The solution might involve quite a difference in our way of life. I do tend to bottle up quite a lot, and that leads to depression as well."

170

Do you think the loss of Abi contributed to that?

"No, I don't think so; it's just the way I am. And it has its ups and downs; it is a family characteristic. My mother was quite a severe depressive and had ECT at one stage. A psychiatrist who was pretty vigorous in the treatment of depression and a fan of drugs prescribed ECT for her. When I was a student I asked him to come and see mother and he agreed that she needed treatment – I don't think she had much in the way of pills, but several sessions of ECT which I think helped her.

She must have been fairly young then – in her 40s and maybe menopausal. My father was a little bit depressed, but then he had a lot to be depressed about working as a tax inspector. He used to have a lot of difficult cases, some of whom lived in the West End of Newcastle where we lived. He used to bring problems home and chew them overnight or over the weekend, not a good thing for family life. Also he had concerns about the church as well, and responsibilities; he gave the church a lot of time and money. Phil has had one or two episodes of depression too."

Was there any advice you wanted to give me and held back from? When you saw how I was behaving or managing since Abi died?

"I don't honestly think so. I suppose I might have given advice if it had been requested or if I felt that you needed something only I could give and perhaps Paddy couldn't give. I could put the question to you – did you feel I could have given you more support or encouragement and you regret I didn't do so?"

It's difficult given what you said about feeling it is a very private process. Looking back, what I might have said

171

was, "Am I doing this OK? In the way I was bringing up the other children, stumbling through".

"I wasn't aware of what was going on later, such as Paddy's vasectomy reversal, fertility treatment, till afterwards."

Did that upset you?

"No, who am I..."

(I assume he would have finished this sentence by saying who am I to poke my nose in etc.)

I know what you mean, but...

"If I was a different person, an extrovert, interfering person like my partner, Rick, I might have said you should do this, that and the other. If I had taken that attitude, you might not have resented it but Paddy would have done. 'She's my wife and I am looking after her.' I never get involved in discussing anything personal with Paddy."

I know that. Having you two as my parents and the role models you are, the messages are "you get on with it, you cope, and be as strong as you can". I feel proud of the way I've got through it and my children but I do wish it could have been different. I think Abi is a taboo subject and I want this to be liberating for people, so my children can talk about her in a way they rarely do. The whole secrecy of afterwards, GIFT (a hugely stressful process to go through), getting pregnant anyway later on, the miscarriage: it was all very difficult and painful. I know if Cathy was going through it I would want to know. Partly because of the self-development work I have done as part of my training, I've been able to work things out and understand more.

I don't think I was sitting there for years wishing you would give me some advice, instead I trusted that you would tell me if you thought I was doing things wrongly. The other thing was I found it hard enough to manage myself and the children and I couldn't have shared other things like the fertility process because the chances were so remote of it working. I didn't want to raise people's hopes, or worry people needlessly.

Has being involved with Quakers helped?

"Very helpful. I think I may have mentioned, not sure which stage it was - maybe just a week or two after Abi died – that I became aware that some women had had a meeting amongst themselves, a private Quaker Meeting of support. I was very conscious after that that I was feeling calmer in myself. I attributed that feeling to the fact they had had this meeting – I got up in Meeting and said so."

Do you believe that if people gather together for a Quaker meeting there is a positive impact on an individual's state of mind then?

"Yes I do. I can't explain it, just a fact, it doesn't happen very often but that's because people don't gather together that often."

That's what we do in Oasis[17]. If someone is in difficulties we do that. And we always have ten minutes quiet time

---

[17] The Oasis School of Human Relations works out of a developmental model which recognises three fundamental elements within any human system: the people, their interaction and the system(s) which contain them. We work with people and their questions, key decision makers, communities and the workplaces of tomorrow. We are the global pioneers in the application and the practice of Whole Person Learning through human relations.

before our Directors' days. It's a way to get rid of the outside world. The inner life is important to us.

"That's interesting. Do you have any more questions?"

The only remaining question I have is what do you think of me doing this?

"I think it's something which will be incredibly useful to the family, quite apart from anyone outside. And I'd have no objection to that – the sort of people who would read the book we wouldn't meet in the ordinary way."

We finished our conversation here and when I listened to the tape later it was an interesting experience; the first sentences when I am trying to put him at his ease seemed to come out in a jumble, and I don't always say quite what I want to say. I tried to put him at his ease because I knew he was slightly ambivalent about the wisdom of my project.

I had thought while we were talking together of how relaxed he looked. He was sitting with his arms up behind his head and appeared quite comfortable in the chair. He sounds so much older when I listen to the recording, yet I don't pick that up to the same extent when I see him. He sounds unsure and the anger he described was the part that surprised me, I really didn't expect that. He sounded angry with Paddy and that must have been buried for such a long time. I never knew about it, I would never have guessed, and I don't know when it disappeared or maybe it just dissipated gradually with time. His comfort has been the strength of the relationship Paddy and I have, that we are so close together, and I can only imagine that if he had ever felt like voicing that anger it could have done irreparable harm to the family relationship.

His anger stayed with me since we talked. Part of this process was about the conversations being confidential, so at the time I had no-one to talk to about how my father felt. Subsequently I talked to Paddy about my father's anger and, as I had suspected, Paddy wasn't surprised and was completely understanding. He knows as well as I do that anger is an important part of the bereavement process. I explained this to my parents, who were very anxious about what had been said. They were worried Paddy would be upset or not understand which could be damaging to their relationship. It was challenging to ensure that they understood how important it was to include those remarks in this book, because those feelings are not unusual ones. To have omitted that section from this chapter would feel incongruent to me.

Ten

Alison

My mother had been such a support to us all every time a baby was born, often being phoned in the middle of the night to come and help. Every time I imagine she would have been through the same procedure – working out what to pack, changing her library books to make sure she had enough to read to keep her going in the evenings. So there was no real reason for her to be apprehensive and think that this time would be much different from the times that went before. I am sure she was glad to be called in to help at a time of illness of one of the children, she was very close to all four of them, she knew where school was, when to collect the children and something of our daily routine.

It's only now as I reflect back to those times, that this might have been a huge challenge for her: coming to live in our house and coping with several lively children when she herself had had just two children to raise. Yet she never once said that she found it hard, or couldn't cope. I could always rely on her utterly.

So when Abi became ill, I turned to her. Thinking back, I don't know quite when I realised that Abi's death had put some kind of a barrier between my mother and me. I don't mean that I could never talk to her or my father, that's not it, but I found it increasingly difficult as the years went by to find a way to communicate my feelings to my parents. And that felt incomprehensible on one level because I have always felt we had a close relationship. I shared a lot of my concerns and anxieties with them about myself and my children as they were growing up, but now this biggest experience that had hit me was something I found impossible to talk about. Partly I think this was because of my way of coping with it, which, of course, was directly related to the way in which I was brought up.

I don't believe this was a 'bad' way to bring me up; there is nothing wrong with encouraging children to be self-sufficient and independent. But I don't think that was quite how it was or all there was to it. After Abi died, my instincts and reactions were telling me to try to get on with life and create some kind of normality again as quickly as I could, for all our sakes. But deep down I think I wanted to be taken care of, and there was an internal battle going on between the child and the adult within me.

Alison (my mother) with Abi (my daughter) the summer before Abi died

My mother's thought was that if they dared to mention Abi's name to Paddy and me, our reaction was that we didn't want to talk about it – we put the shutters up straightaway. They talked to each other about her and what had happened and about the fact that they couldn't talk naturally to us about it, was there anything they could do about it? Over the years they talked a lot, and still do.

Her memories of that time were very vivid. At the time we spoke she was 79 years old and occasionally struggled to remember people's names, what happened when and so on. But her memories of this time are extremely clear.

"Paddy rang and asked me to come down to Hull because Abi was very ill. I thought to myself, yes, but it'll be OK. I never thought it would go onto that, more that it'll take a while to get her back and fit again – you'll need some help. It never occurred to me until I got there. I changed my library books before I came down, thinking – and telling myself – it's not that bad, put it out of your mind. It'll just be a very difficult time.

It was when I got to the hospital that I began to realise. Maggie took me in the afternoon; she was very clear about her taking me. I thought it was a bit odd at the time, because I could have driven myself. I remember going into a waiting room at the side of the ward. I wasn't sure what was going to happen, then you rushed in and said, 'Oh Mummy I am so sorry, I can't tell you what it's like, it's very bad and I'm so sorry'. You were very upset. That's when I realised it was really bad. I waited a while and then Paddy came to get me and took me in to see Abi. You were sitting with her and she was on a pillow on your lap – I remember it vividly. I looked at her and she didn't look too bad but I sensed how bad it was. I remember it so well. I was trying to get my head round this – I thought: pull yourself together, there are three children to pick up from school and they'll need feeding."

Of course, there was no-one for you to talk to then?

"There was nobody to talk to, no. In the schoolyard as I was waiting for the children the next day, I was the centre of attention as people kept away – looking at me but standing away and not speaking, clearly talking amongst themselves. I thought, gosh, they obviously know. The children came out and we went straight down to the hospital. I remember driving down and talking normally and keeping a normal conversation going. When we got there, we had to put on gowns and slippers, this is a memory as clear as crystal. I put Simon's on for him; it was trailing on the ground because it was far too big and so were the shoes. He said it was silly, 'It's far too big and the shoes are far too big'. I thought to myself that's because they were never meant for a little boy like you."

Did the children ask you any questions?

"No, they didn't ask, we talked about normal things, about going to see Abi, and that Daddy and Mummy will be there. Paddy came and went from home to the hospital to try and keep some normality for them. The next day Abi had changed – I could see the difference in her."

Like she was going really?

"Yes, she had changed – earlier I had thought she will be OK. It was ignorance, or hopefulness that she would be OK. That second day she wasn't. I remember Matthew standing beside her with his tears dropping onto Abi's arm – it was so hard. Simon was OK and Cathy was very controlled; Matthew was very quiet and holding her hand and the tears were just dropping onto her. What do you say? It was very hard to know what to say. Matthew realised. I think she had little squares on her eyes[18] and

---

[18] Unconscious patients often have squares of gauze over their eyes to protect them from any damage.

I knew then that she's not going to make it. Daddy came that Friday – and Marley[19] came too."

Did you ring Daddy then and talk to him?

"Yes, I did speak to him. I remember one of your friends rang me one afternoon. I was trying to make some food. I got a headache and it was a blinding migraine – never had one like it since. I remember I was so sick on the carpet by the phone. I had to say I have to go to pick up the children up, and of course I had to clear up the sick and wash the floor! Cleaning up the floor made me feel better. I've never forgotten it – whenever I came back to the house I remembered it. I suppose it was an accumulation of all the stress, but it was a real blinder."

Do you remember being in the room when the neurosurgeon came out to speak to us? Do you remember what he said?

"Maybe I wasn't there? He came out and said something like Abi's dead. Paddy had been with them doing the tests on her brain. No, I wasn't there."

(She was adamant about this, but my memory is that we were all there, the room felt so crowded to me, but also I was so relieved that we were all together and we didn't have to tell anyone else what had happened.)

"He was very, very blunt – no room for any argument here. No hope.

Daddy came by train on the Friday – I thought he should have come the day before but he had to work. Maybe he

---

19 Marley was Paddy's mother.

181

didn't realise, or didn't want to. Afterwards you think
– but you don't want to realise. The first day I thought she
would be all right."

So the last time you saw her she had those little squares
on her eyes?

"You'd had her on your lap all the time, nursing her. My
concern was for you, as well – how can I help them? I
find it very difficult to say things when there's big, big
trouble – I retreat, I can cope with the practical, but saying
things... I find it so hard."

Were there things you wanted to say but you stopped
yourself?

"I think so. I felt I wanted to say to you how much it meant,
and how much you meant. It was so – just to see you
suffering so much. It was the hardest thing I've known."

I suppose it was several things, you seeing me suffering,
losing Abi and also the effect on the children.

"Seeing Matthew cry, I never forget it. Silent, tears
dropping, it was the worst thing I've ever seen. I'm not
surprised he finds it hard to talk about it because he was
so close to her."

That Friday evening Cathy went to her ballet class. I
don't know how on earth anyone made that decision, but
obviously we must have thought it might be a good idea.

"Matthew went too with Marley but they never found it.
I don't know how anyone thought that was a good idea.
The cars were at the hospital, and I remember thinking this
is crazy when I drove out. I drove over a kerb. I was very

upset and I remember reversing back. It was dark, maybe raining; awful weather. I knew the way back home, then Marley came and we thought, 'What shall we do'."

What was it like for you and Marley – did you two talk together?

"Yes we did but I can't remember what we said. She said, 'What shall we do, we need food for the children'. Marley said she would cook pasta; we ended up with bowls full! I cooked mince."

Can you remember if she said how she felt?

"I don't think she did say. Her concern was for you: wondering how you would cope with this. I said she will, she is very strong, she will cope. Marley said Paddy and Christine are so close – I think that will help."

She didn't mention how she felt then, but maybe you didn't either?

"No, I don't think I did. My concern throughout was that the only way I could get through this is by being practical: I've got to feed the children, get them to bed. I think Paddy came home to see them on the Thursday, the night before Abi died, and get them to bed.

Marley went off to try and find the ballet class with the pair of them, and I thought, 'This is crazy. I don't know where she is going!' I had Simon with me.

Am I rambling?"

No, no – the memories seem to be coming thick and fast.

"It was awful weather that evening and time was getting on. I know Daddy was there, but I don't know how, I didn't see him. I didn't see him till after she died. I remember being in the kitchen, it seemed like a long way from there to the front door. Is this upsetting you?"

I've blotted a lot out, there's a lot I've pushed away.

"Marley and I were in the kitchen, the front door had opened and you came in first, you had that quilt that Audrey made for Abi over your arm and something else (her dressing gown I think). You came in, Paddy behind and Anthony at the back. I looked at Anthony and I knew perfectly well. You came and marched quickly and firmly into the kitchen. I went forward to say, 'Didi,[20] what's happened, how are you?' You said you were all right, 'What about the children?'

Marley was back by that time, because they never found ballet. I tried to get through to you and said the children needed to have their meal. We were all at different places; there was no connection between any of us. We couldn't connect. It didn't seem possible. We couldn't sit down and talk – no way, there was nothing we could say, it was all so dreadful. We were like different people. The important thing was to feed the children. Whether you took the children off and talked to them, I don't know."

(My mother filled in the gaps for me here, between the time when the neurosurgeon came and told us all that Abi had died, and Paddy and I getting back to our house without her.)

---

[20] 'Didi' refers to me. When I was little I couldn't pronounce Christine. My parents still often call me Didi and Paddy adopted it too.

You went back home to Newcastle then and then drove back to Hull for the funeral and then again for the meeting we held to celebrate her life.

"On the day after she died, we didn't know what to do. We felt, I felt in my heart, you would be better with just your own family but I didn't want to appear to be leaving you."

To abandon me?

"If we could help we would have, however you came and said, 'You two should go back.' I was glad. I felt it was the right thing. We came back home to Newcastle."

Was it hard to leave me?

"Very hard, Daddy was driving and I cried all the way back up the motorway. Didn't know what I was doing, what to do or what could I do? I can't remember but we must have rung Rosalind at some point."

The other thing was you must have had contact with Phil at that time.

"Phil feels he should have come back from New Zealand, he bitterly regrets it. But he was in a mess with his own family at the time.

He said to me, 'I think I should have come back, it was awful the day of the funeral. I should have been there.' He felt he let you down.

I don't feel that at all.

**The family in Northumberland when Phil
and his first wife were over from New Zealand**

*"We came back and had to tell people. I remember going
to the butcher; Daddy was working and I had to feed him.
I saw Naomi, a friend, who had lost a little girl when they
lived in Brussels. Her mother took the children out for a
walk, and one of them was knocked down and killed. Her
mother lived to a ripe old age. Naomi said, 'I haven't seen
you – have you been away?' I had to tell her, she was so
upset because she knew exactly what it was like."*

When you described people in the playground at school
and you being the centre of attention, in Hull lots of people
knew or knew something was happening. In Newcastle
people wouldn't know at all.

*"We had lots of letters from all sorts of people. They are
here if you'd like them? They were from people expressing
their love to us, and to you."*

When you came back, were there particular friends you could talk to?

"Not really, though perhaps Audrey because she was a neighbour and then she told people. Sue was in tears, very upset and emotional. Quakers knew; they had a special meeting and prayers. They talked about your wedding there and what you were going through."

But you weren't at Meeting for that?

"No, we just heard about it. People were very kind."

Did that kind of thing help?

"Not at the time really. Looking back now, it was very thoughtful. All I felt was apprehension about the funeral. How are we going to get through this?

I remember I was so cack-handed that day. There was a little posy of flowers on the bench in the kitchen and I didn't know where it had come from. I said something about it, and I don't know what you said. I didn't realise, should I have brought some flowers? We hadn't done. Looking back now – why not? Everything was all so awful and jumbled. I found it hard to know what to do: never mind my grief, I needed to do things to help you. I was so concerned about you. Felt I couldn't ask what sort of funeral will it be? Was it going to be a Quaker one?"

Do you think I was pushing you away?

"No, it was too personal a question, it was silly. There was no-one to speak. Not like a Quaker funeral or meeting. Seeing the three children with Paddy, and us sitting behind with Marley – it was the hardest thing I have known. Not

like when my mother or my grandmother died, nothing was as bad as this."

(Her voice sounded very worn here, very tired.)

"I have very vivid memories. The music was Elgar, Nimrod. I was sitting in the back, thinking, this is just so awful. I can't believe it. I remember I breathed, and I heard myself catching my breath and I said to myself shut up, stop it. I don't know if anyone else heard. You walked forward with the posy of flowers; it was very hard to see. I've never talked about it to anyone. I remember thinking how hard it is to see your daughter going through this. You were so strong and calm with the posy and when you walked back. I have never known anything so painful – do you remember that?"

I can remember it – I can remember how cold it felt, how numb I felt – my whole body felt like it had shut down.

"We all went in Paddy's car, the Space Cruiser. We waited at the crematorium outside for the hearse to come. A child's funeral, when it's your own family it's very hard to bear; it's a very vivid memory."

Looking back it seems mad the way we tried to pack such a lot in: the funeral on the Wednesday and the celebration meeting on the Saturday. So close together. Somehow we must have told you what we were going to do. Do you have any thoughts about that?

"That this is going to be hard. But they've thought it's better to do it now. One thing that sticks in my mind from that celebration meeting is that I was sitting with Marley and you had some flowers on a table in the window. You and Paddy were sitting together – Cathy read a poem,

which I've got written down in a book I'll show you. A very happy book! And another poem that Lydia Ramage said to me. She sat down after Quakers one morning next to me and recited it to me in her quavery voice. It was very hard."

(I went and found her Commonplace book[21] and we had a look at it.)

Did things like that help?

"Yes, oh yes. I remember sitting up in the bedroom one afternoon and reading some poetry and thinking – if only that door would open and she would run in and cross to the window. I remember sitting there so well – I just wanted that door to open and her to run in."

Has she ever come?

"No, but I thought then that I sensed her that day. Am I mad? I thought I'll keep watching the door and wait for her."

Was that long after?

"No, not long, probably sometime the next year.

The celebration meeting was a very sunny day; the room full of people and children and I remember you saying that we need to start. Your old friends, the Plunketts, had been delayed but people were getting restless."

Sue read something in the meeting, which I think was the Owl and the Pussycat. She sang as well, she started that off for people to join in. One of the songs we sang

---

[21]   See page 229.

was a lullaby for the children, which we used to sing to them before they went to sleep:

"Row, row, row your boat
Gently down the stream
Merrily, merrily, merrily
Life is but a dream."

"You'd asked Matthew to read something but he said he couldn't. Cathy said she would – that was very hard to listen to. I remember that after a little while Marley took my hand."

(It was very unusual for Marley to show her feelings, and Alison was upset here as she described it to me.)

"Then I remember feeling I needed to get out of the room, I got up and went out into the pantry and Annie followed me – I was in tears. She was so nice to me, I've never forgotten that. I was upset, not sobbing. She talked to me then."

I think we asked Daddy to read something from the Prophet. The bit about children not being yours, they are just on loan.

Did you think the children understood what had happened?

"I think they did but I think they didn't understand just what it meant. They knew what had happened."

Did you know what it meant?

"Yes, I think so – I have a bit of a morbid streak in me. Such an event shapes all the rest of your life and I worried about the effect on you and the family. I wondered if you would get very depressed, although I didn't think you

would – you're very strong. I thought about how awful it would be if you were depressed, and would you talk about it, because you didn't talk to us about how you felt."

Did you wish I had?

"Not at the time, but a little later. I wished we could talk about it."

Did you ever think of plonking me down in a chair and saying we need to talk about this?

"I felt you and Paddy were so close. I felt he would have resented it."

It would have been a hard thing to have done, to have got me in a corner. It would have taken a lot from me.

"Maybe I should have done."

The 'what ifs' interest me. If you have a thought like that, what is it that stops you?

"I felt it's going to make it worse, as if anything could, or would it matter anyway? Would it be upsetting? I wanted to cope with things, not to make it worse for you. You were my concern, more than the children. I felt I could cope with this, but I wanted to protect you. It was very hard to see you, it was obvious what you were going through but you weren't saying."

When I look at photos of the year afterwards, I look like a ghost.

"There's one where you are sitting on the sofa and you look so tense. I just didn't want to make it worse."

You couldn't make it better. What did that do to you?
There sounds like a lot of conflict.

*"I was a bit scared of Paddy – not 'scared scared' but he
could have reacted in any way, because he was suffering
too. I was frightened that he would say, just don't talk
about it, don't say anything."*

Did you feel angry at all?

"No, never, never."

So you weren't angry that it had happened, or that Abi
hadn't been looked after, or angry with me, or Paddy?

*"No, not at all, I remember you saying that they hadn't
had some equipment there and I felt oh, that's so bad, to
think – would it have made a difference? But I don't know
what it was."*

The main thing was the doctor who was incompetent and
put the airway into the wrong place.

"We didn't know that."

He has had to live with that forever too. They never had
proper resuscitation equipment. The children's ward
was a long way away and it always took anaesthetists
a long time to get there in a crisis. So really it was a
systems failure.

"Did they learn?"

No, I've got it in my head that it happened again, but I'm
not sure if that's right.

"You said Paddy felt like giving up? He was so upset about the carelessness. He must have felt angry, was he angry about that?"

When we met Elspeth, the consultant, Paddy shouted at her and I felt very uncomfortable, even though I knew he had to get it off his chest. Elspeth just sat there and took it. I imagine she knew it was important for him to express his anger in that way, and then she advised us to sue the hospital. Paddy and I talked about it but thought it would be too difficult. What good would it do? Nothing would bring Abi back; we would have our name all over the papers, plus Paddy had to continue to work there. Perhaps we should have done, now that we look back. It would have channelled some energy, maybe prevented other deaths. I think Paddy getting rid of that anger must have helped him then. I kept mine inside me for years.

"We realised something was wrong with the hospital, that something wasn't there. Daddy wondered how Paddy could go on. Maggie said Abi was walking down the stairs before she went into hospital. They were round at your house that afternoon."

In the hospital, she wanted to go for a wee so I said I would carry her but she insisted on walking. She wouldn't be carried – she was stubborn.

"What happened to make her deteriorate?"

She came back and sat on my knee. It was late and I was trying to keep her awake because I knew the doctor was going to come and start sticking needles into her. She was just getting so tired. The doctor came and couldn't get a needle into a vein, she just went quiet and

193

stopped breathing. I don't know if it was the shock or the combination of the tiredness and her swollen throat. It's very simple really.

Paddy thinks if it had been at home he would have done a tracheotomy. Whether he would or not, I don't know and it's irrelevant anyway – what happened has happened. One of my questions is why did it happen to us as a family, why to her? I've tried to understand and make sense of it and I've often thought about it.

"I couldn't believe that she had died; she was such a strong little girl, a little toughie. She wasn't like the other three. She had a different character and personality. In her short time she made so much of an impression on everyone who knew her."

Such a lot of people said what a strong personality she had both before and after she died.

What were the worst times since then? It sounds like it gradually got better? I think it's about learning to live with it, not coming to terms. What have been the triggers for the bad times?

*"I don't know. It was very bad at one stage – the first year, thinking this is the most awful thing that I (never mind anyone else) have ever known. Feeling **real heartache**. Really experiencing what that is."*

Did you make any connection with your breast cancer later on?

"No, I didn't think of that – though it was only a couple of years afterwards. I remember the physical pain of her loss; she's not here and she's never going to be here. Also

194

*it's not fair on my daughter. Never mind me – yes, there is me, but **my daughter.***"

(I was so aware of her love and care for me as she spoke then.)

"Someone said to me that they were surprised we hadn't gone off to New Zealand to live. I thought – I would never do that! I couldn't do that."

You sound amazed that anyone should have thought that – yet Phil is there.

"I just couldn't. It would be leaving you and memories of Abi. No way, no way. That possibility never crossed either of our minds."

I wonder about birthdays, anniversaries, your Golden Wedding, do those times feel more poignant because she isn't here?

"Yes, not my birthday, but her birthday, and the day she died. That time of year I think of her more. I always used to take freesias to Quakers on the nearest Sunday to 16th November, then I used to sit in Meeting and look at them and feel all the feelings again. I stopped because we were away one year and I've not done it for a few years. Maybe I'd done it enough."

(She was upset again here.)

Do you think that sometimes making a point of feeling those feelings again could be quite helpful? You can see if you've moved on; what greater understanding you have now.

"Yes, I think that's right. When my mother died, I just had feelings of guilt – I pushed those way, way back."

Can you remember Cathy talking to you and saying it was her fault because she had had a cold and not been well?

"Yes, that comes back, I'd forgotten that."

What was it like having to come back to Hull, visiting us in the house later on?

"After the funeral – that first Christmas was hard. We weren't going to come then you said I think you should come."

I really wanted you to come so that we were all together, but I know it was hard for me to say it as clearly as that.

"We went to Spring Street Theatre to a Christmas show for children; that was just something to do. I remember little about that Christmas. Phil had sent a parcel with something in for Abi. I kept it at home and it's still upstairs – a little wooden toy."

I always thought you found it hard coming past the hospital.

"Yes I did, I remember driving down that road. I didn't like it."

Were you relieved when we moved house?

"Yes, but then on the other hand, when I went back to that house, I could see her little fingermarks going up the stairs. I'd put my hand on them walking up, and I could see her walking up and down. I remember her so vividly saying to Simon when he'd been naughty and he'd been"

told he would be put out, 'You out'! She was shouting and pointing at him; sitting in her highchair in full command. She was very funny for a little girl."

(We were able to laugh about this together, which was so nice, it felt so unusual, a release and the liberation I was wanting. It was us remembering together with affection for Abi, and for each other and the memories we shared.)

"Later the next year the children were staying with us and we went to Rothbury (no, it wasn't Rothbury, it was Warkworth) and took photos of the three of them. We went to the church there and had an ice cream. We went in and someone was playing the organ. I looked round and Simon rushed out and ran off. I ran after him; he was sitting outside crying. I thought I was stupid; I shouldn't have done it; I never thought. He didn't cry a lot, then we went and had an ice cream and took some photos: they were the first ones we had taken with just the three children. Perhaps the organ music reminded him of the funeral; it wasn't the same music but it was some sort of trigger."

When you meet new people and they ask about family and so on, how do you answer them?

"It is easier than it was. I say that we've got quite a few grandchildren: there are the three older ones, and the New Zealand ones. People in Newcastle know of you of course, medical people and so on. I always say that, well, actually Paddy and Christine had four children but the youngest little girl died. They say, 'Oh how dreadful', and then don't quite know what to say."

Have you always said it?

"Always, I don't want her missed out. I've said to Daddy if I die, when he puts the notice in the paper I want my grandchildren mentioned and it must include 'Always remembering Abigail'. He says rather impatiently, 'Oh yes, yes!' But it is very important to me. I might be here forever, of course! Though I doubt it!

You've talked about your faith and how you don't really feel like you have a spiritual home. I wondered if Abi's death had affected your faith, what it had done to your faith. Did you pray?

"Yes, when she died I did. I don't think of it as Quakers, just something personal. I suppose it was to God but not to an Anglican being. A personal thing: how am I going to get through this? Please help me through this. How will I cope with this, feeding these little children, how am I going to cope with their feelings?

It was like driving up to Dundee to visit you, when you were about to give birth but you had broken your arm. Knowing it was going to be difficult, wondering how you would breastfeed. All the way up, I was working it all out. I told myself – she will have worked it out and know how to cope, it'll be fine. There was a Service for the Queen Mother for her 80th birthday in 1980 on the radio as I was driving. One of the main things in the service was 'all will be well and all manner of things shall be well'. Not sure where it comes from. I thought, that's interesting, I've never heard that before. I took it as being a message because it was very strong: all manner of things shall be well.

I got to Dundee and unpacked, then Paddy came to the kitchen, shut the door, stood there and said, 'The baby's dead'. This cannot be true. I felt like saying to 'God', 'So,

198

you've let me down. I've come all this way believing that it would be OK and it's not OK at all'. That was hard, but not as hard as this.

You were so poorly, I remember leaving the house when I was going home and going to get petrol, I had tears in my eyes and the man put the petrol in the car for me. I stopped at Kirkwhelpington to see Sue – they were pleased to see me, because they had been wondering what had been happening. I thought that was bad, but it was nothing compared to losing Abi."

I have wondered about how we communicated with one another over that experience. I didn't know you went to see Sue then and I don't know what happened about telling the rest of Paddy's family.

You said you talked to Daddy a lot and I wondered if anyone has helped you through the process? Did he help or was it too difficult to help each other?

"Not really, no-one really helped. He finds it so hard to... he's sympathetic, very kind but I don't think he realises quite how women feel. Women have a different outlook. He would do anything for me, help in any way. He'd say, 'Now try not to get upset, don't think about it.' But that's not the answer – you want to be upset."

So you want to talk about it?

"Yes."

Two of your very close friends have died over the last few years. After Dorothy died, I remember you saying that she was your best friend.

"I trusted her. I talked to both of them. And other friends too, people who knew you and were so concerned for you. There wasn't anyone at Quakers I was close enough to apart from Lydia. I remember her saying she thought I shouldn't attend Meeting when they had the children in. That was quite soon afterwards."

Did Marley talk to you at all later on? Voice her concerns or talk about Abi to you?

"Yes, but she was never very personal about Abi. She never really talked to me about her; she wasn't that kind of woman. I mention Abi to people, but maybe not as much now."

You and Marley were both mothers, you must both have been suffering in your own ways and you both had children who were suffering, so you had a united experience but not the close relationship to share it.

"I can't remember her ever saying anything. I do remember her once saying, 'Why did Gerald stay with me, because I've always been difficult – I've been a tricky person to be married to'. That's as personal as she ever was."

The influence that Abi had – have you ever thought about her destiny, what she was here for? What was the point of her being born?

"I've often wondered what Abi would be doing now. I felt she was so strong – how good she would have been for the others, even though she was the youngest. I can't imagine what she would have done. She was very different from Cathy."

The times the kids have been to stay with you on their own, have you ever talked about Abi then?

"We often mentioned her but never really talked or went anywhere. I thought they are too upset – it's too private."

We kept Paddy having a reversal of his vasectomy and going on to have GIFT a secret until I got pregnant. When we told you I was pregnant, you were just about to go to New Zealand on holiday and to see Phil and I had the miscarriage while you were away. What was that like? We had decided another baby was the only thing that would make the pain a bit better – what did you think?

"I was very apprehensive, and worrying about whether it was a good idea to go off to New Zealand, as well as worrying in case when you had the baby it turned out that something was wrong with it. How sad that would be if that happened. My main concern was for you."

Then I got pregnant again later on of course. Did you think we were being a bit stupid then?

"No, I could understand it, but remember thinking, 'Have they thought this through?' Daddy said, 'Of course they have, they would find out earlier if there was something wrong with the baby.' Can never replace Abi; no way. But I do know what you mean. I felt it was a lot to take on: to have another child in your 40s and with the other children being the ages they were; you had been through so much. I was very protective of you.

Matthew's birth wasn't that much fun, Cathy's was tricky, and Simon's – nothing has been easy for you. I felt you had been through enough. I felt relieved, I know it sounds cruel but I am being honest! How hard it would have been for you with a disabled baby, so sad."

Just one more thing, what do you think about me doing this?

"As soon as I heard about it, I thought it was a good idea. Daddy was unsure, because it would bring back a lot of sad memories."

It's been so good, it has helped me; you've reminded me about things, told me things I didn't know.

"It's like a little film in my head. It's never moved or gone away."

We stopped our conversation at this point; we had been talking for a long time and were both getting tired. I reflected a little later that it had been a cathartic experience for us both. She said she was nervous about it beforehand, but found it a great thing to have done. It was so helpful for me to be able to fill in some of the holes in my memory, to understand more about how it had been for my mother, and to bridge the gap between us whenever Abi's name was mentioned.

A couple of weeks later we were talking on the phone one morning, and Mum asked me how the book was going, I told her how many words I had written and she was amazed!

We talked a little about the process and I said that I was not finding it that upsetting but that it was very tiring. It was another reminder of the tiring nature of grief as I remembered all over again how exhausted I used to feel even though I had done nothing really. Just having to get through the days one by one was so hard, and my difficulty in sleeping has persisted to this day. It would be wonderful to think that with the completion of this book, I might begin to sleep through the night!

She said she remembered that, from the week after Abi died, she felt she had to phone me every morning. She needed to hear my voice and I wondered if it was something like her needing to hear I was still alive (though she didn't say that; it was more what was underneath her words) then she could try and get on with her day. She knew her phoning me wasn't helping, by the tone of my voice and how I said whatever I did say I guess, but it was something she needed to do. She realised she had to stop ringing so much and I am sure she found this hard to do, but she did it for me. She allowed me the space I needed to fumble my way through the grief and sadness in my own way.

I had forgotten this, but could vaguely remember something like that happening and I know I did find it difficult to talk. I imagine I felt I needed to sound OK, when I didn't feel it. I would have tried to make it all right for her, when I could hear she was so upset. It was so difficult to talk about the emotional distance between us then, and she wasn't able to explain why she was ringing me.

Our conversation brought home the loneliness of what it was like for my mother around the time of Abi's illness and death in a way I had never considered before. As we talked further, I began to realise what it was like for her then. That when she left us at the hospital that day, she was all on her own, she had to drive to the children's schools and pick them up, take them back to our home, then look after the children in my house, using my kitchen and so on. She played such an important part in caring for the children, keeping some kind of normal life continuing for them during this completely out-of-the-ordinary situation. She had no-one to talk to because Paddy was with Abi and me.

What also struck me as I listened to the tape of our conversation was her faith and belief in me; that I would be able to cope through the two big crises of my life. In 1980 when I was in the midst of having an operation on my arm and giving birth, she was quite sure I would have worked out how I would breastfeed a baby whilst having an arm in plaster from shoulder to wrist. The poignancy for me was how my mother had such faith in the strength of the message she had heard on her journey up to Dundee (about all being well, and all manner of things shall be well), but was so let down by what actually happened. It made me wonder if that was the first time she felt let down by the God, or spiritual being, she believed in.

It also gave me another insight into what it's like being a mother. That for many women, they are there to be called on in a crisis, and they simply get on with doing what needs to be done. If they don't talk about how hard it is for themselves to anyone, they will be ignored and left to get on with it, and yet they are suffering, doing the best they can in impossible circumstances. I can put myself into her shoes; I would do just the same, of course. And I know I would want someone to be there for me, to help me whilst I am doing my level best for my child.

I didn't feel upset about her talking and remembering. It was all helping, putting the bigger picture together so that I knew what was going on for other people. I was so isolated and alone through it all; the only person I really felt I was with, the only person I wanted to be with was Abi. I felt more alone than I had ever felt in my life.

I am so glad I created the opportunity for her to talk to me and describe it all again. She mentioned at one point about how it was like a film that played on a loop round and round her mind for a long time after Abi died. My mother is so talented at describing situations – they become a vivid picture. The part when she talked about Simon being cross with the size of the gowns and shoes they were expected to wear when going into Intensive Care to see Abi was such a poignant picture. I could just see this little boy of six, a very solid little chap with white-blond hair who thought the whole thing was ridiculous. Of course, this was one thing I didn't know about because we were already in the ward with Abi.

When she was filling in some of the gaps in my memory and knowledge of that awful night, I learned that the Grannies took the children back home while Paddy and I stayed at the hospital to have one last time of being with Abi before they took her away. I have little memory of how long we spent with her then but we said our goodbyes at that point. I suspect as soon as I had done that I resolved that my next priority was to get back to the older three and comfort them, explain more if they had questions and have some time together as a family of five. I am sure that underneath what I needed for myself was the comfort of being with them, of having children's arms around me, hugging me tight. I would never have that from Abi again.

I can remember the feelings I had that Friday evening when Abi had died, as my mother described what I did and how I behaved as I came back to the house. I felt completely disconnected from reality; I hadn't been in the house for four days. My entire life had changed in that time-span. I had walked out of the house the mother of four, and come back with one of my children having died.

I had to come back to be the mother of the three children I had left and learn how to look after them through this huge experience. I needed to get back into control again. I had lost control over those four days and I had to get back in touch with my children somehow. The only way I knew to do that was to do the practical things. That, of course, was the link with my mother, her way of coping and the way in which I had been brought up.

My mother keeps the Commonplace book she talked about in her dressing table drawer along with some reminders of Abi. There is a lock of her hair in that drawer along with one of her little socks that we left behind after one of our visits. I picture my mother in her bedroom, in the afternoon with the light fading, thinking about Abi and me, remembering times when we came to stay, what Abi would have been doing, seeing her in the house, remembering what she would have been playing with.

My mother would be crying maybe, reading poetry or perhaps hearing something on the radio that inspired her to find the source and write it down. My imagination lets me picture her sitting there, thinking and thinking about what had happened, not knowing what to do for the best, wanting to help me, perhaps feeling hurt because I was pushing her away, feeling so desperately unhappy and powerless to do anything to help.

This is one of my big regrets, that through it all I was unable to ask for help, that I pushed her away and tried to manage on my own. Yet I can also see that this was the biggest test of my life – this was the moment when I needed to grow up, to become an adult and learn what I needed to learn. I had to do that on my own. I did it, but there was a price to pay. I believe that the process of talking about Abi for this book has been a therapeutic one for both of us and I hope it will continue to be something that bonds rather than separates us.

Reading the pieces in her Commonplace book was immensely powerful for me and the selection in the Appendix gives immense comfort to me. The first time I was transcribing them 'Silent Night' was playing on the radio. I was in tears as I was typing with a combination of emotions from the depth of what I was reading, hearing the simple, beautiful music, and imagining what my mother was going through as she wrote down these words in precise italic handwriting in her book.

Many of the extracts just say it all. Poets have an art of summing up and yet conveying so much in a few lines. As I read, I am able to feel that someone else understands the dreadful situation I found myself in, and to believe that there is light, that at some point I will be able to move on, to remember Abi with joy because she was alive and with us, and not despair because she died too soon. That was what Paddy and I aimed for, what we tried to explain to the children at various stages (even very soon after she died). I am unsure at what point we reached it. But I know now that I can do that, and have been able to do so for some time.

The first poem in this selection was read to Alison one Sunday morning after Quaker Meeting by an old friend, Lydia Ramage. Lydia was a stalwart of Newcastle Meeting and when she contributed in Meeting she would speak directly from the heart in a quavery, light voice. She was able to command attention from the whole of Meeting despite her apparent frailness. She often aimed her thoughts at the children of the Meeting. On this occasion, she took my mother to one side, held her hand and recited this short poem (I imagine she was facing her and looking into her eyes as she spoke the lines). I can picture this scene and imagine the intensity of it, almost that Lydia was willing the thoughts into my mother, forcing her to listen to her and hear what was in the words.

Every time I read these words, I marvel that the selection sums up the pain, the wonderful sense of love in having had Abi, the process of losing her, leaving her behind as my life continued, taking her with me inside me for all time. My mother has the sensitivity, intuition and intelligence to put something together that I think is such a complementary addition to my book.

My mother keeps her wisdom hidden so much of the time – but when she shares it with me, it is wonderful. It connects me with her in such a deep way, I feel so fortunate to have her as my mother.

Our conversations made me think more about the relationship between mothers and daughters, and what a complex one it is. As a daughter, I know that my mother wants to protect me, to stop things hurting. It doesn't seem to matter how old I am, that's part of her make-up as a mother. As a mother myself, I know I am very similar. The challenge was to find a way to let go; let my children make their own mistakes, work things out for themselves.

If my daughter is hurting, what do I do? I may want to rush in and sort things out, as perhaps I did when she was a small child at school. But if she is an adult, I need to let her go. My hurt may feel doubled because I have lost my child; my daughter is small no longer and doesn't need me in the same way. My mother had the loss of her granddaughter as well as her daughter's hurt and distress. She was brilliant at getting on with all the practical things which need doing for a family to function, and yet there is also a place for sitting and being with, letting the tide of feelings overwhelm, overtake. That is one of my regrets: that my mother and I didn't have that time together to let that happen. Until now, that is.

Eleven

January 2009
Anthony and Alison: a Postscript

The experience of talking to my parents was wonderful, though it was clearly hard and extremely tiring for both of them. The end result was that it did feel freer, both at the time and later. We have all been able to talk about Abi much more easily. My mother really helped to fill in the picture, because she had such brilliant recall for much of what had happened and vivid descriptions. I was able to say that one reason for getting on with this is because I want them both to be able to read it so that they know more about what losing Abi had meant for all of us. Each conversation included laughter at some point.

My parents read their chapters and contributions before Christmas 2008. I think there were surprises for both of them; in particular for my mother when she read about the anger my father had felt. She phoned me saying how worried he was about what he had said. I think this was one of the downsides to the long gap between our conversations and me feeling able to ask them to read what I had written. The way in which I structured the process meant I wanted to have all the different conversations and do as much writing as I could before asking any of the family to read their chapters and make comments. I hope I was able to reassure her that I understood about his anger. Feeling angry is a normal part of mourning and the bereavement process. She was anxious that Paddy would be very upset when he read it, but I hope I was able to get her to understand that Paddy knows as much about how people feel at different points in the bereavement process as I do.

My father's reaction when I spoke to him was to suggest we talk face to face over Christmas. He told me that he hadn't realised the whole story and that therefore made a difference to his feelings. He thought that if he had known at the time about the medical mismanagement, he wouldn't have been angry with Paddy. I am still unsure whether he realises that that was part of the purpose for me, why I wanted to embark on this 'project', which he describes as incredibly brave. Why was it that it took 24 years for him to get all the facts? What was it that got in the way of him asking? I did ask him these questions, but at almost 85 his overriding need is to keep things quiet, not to rock the boat, or upset anyone. He did say that he felt if he had asked the questions at the time it would have been intrusive. And, as time progressed, it became more and more difficult.

His other thoughts were about the conflict between being a doctor and a father. This echoed Paddy's description too: the tendency to analyse what is happening; to make sense of things; to understand from the other professionals' point of view.

He also made a comment about Abi's funeral and there being no words; nothing was said, we just had music playing and even that was the wrong movement. He said how discordant the lack of words was with the child that she was. How she loved to talk, sing and so on. I think that was such a good point to make, and one that had never struck me at the time or since. It was another occasion when we rushed to get things sorted out, rather than waiting to think through more clearly what we wanted. Although we might have had to wait 20 years to know what we really wanted, in 1984 we didn't think we had that luxury of time.

My mother's other amazement was my description of him as being very relaxed as he sat "at ease with his hands behind his head". She said this was the complete reverse of how he would be feeling; he never sits like that normally and she thought that it demonstrated that he was, in fact, very ill at ease indeed. She knows him so well, that I took what she said as being true. For me, this was another indication of how my parents are willing to put themselves through discomfort for me.

The process also had the effect of helping my mother talk about other deaths in her life. She talked to me about the death of her grandmother, who looked after her as a child; she remembered someone coming up to her at her grandmother's funeral and telling her, "You have lost the best friend you will ever have," and how she had cried then.

She also talked about the death of her own mother in 1952 following a fall and how she had felt she had to cope by being very strong and not letting any feelings show on the surface.

She described the differences between the way she remembered the events surrounding Abi's death compared with my father's memories: she could see how emotional her descriptions were, that for her the whole thing is still very vivid and on the surface. She told me about when my grandfather died; how my father had rushed to his office when he got the message my grandfather had collapsed. When he arrived he realised his father had had a coronary thrombosis. He gave him some morphine and arranged for him to go into hospital and then he himself went back to the practice and continued with his surgery.

His father died later that day in hospital and it was something that preyed on my father's mind for many years. My grandmother was in the midst of her baking day, and had different mixtures in bowls and basins around her kitchen. Somehow she managed to get all these down to our house and continued with her baking in my mother's kitchen. I find this such a difficult concept – my grandmother couldn't drive, so I don't understand how she got the three miles to our house. How did she pack all the ingredients into baskets and so on to bring with her? How could she concentrate on something like that when her husband was in hospital? Why didn't she want to go and be with him?

My mother said that no-one then ever talked about feelings, everyone just got on with life and work and didn't let anything interfere; even deaths it seems.

Yet perhaps this is no more strange than someone thinking it would be a good idea for Cathy to go to ballet the night her little sister had died and her granny to drive her to the other side of Hull, with no idea of the route, relying on another traumatised child of 11 to help her find the way!

It makes me wonder the extent to which we carry all those deaths and losses within ourselves. Perhaps a positive aspect of this process is that my parents have been able to let go a little, to talk to me so that I can understand more about their history.

My mother went on to describe to me what it was like to live in a small village in Northumberland in the 1930s and 40s, with her grandmother, who was the midwife as well as the person who laid out the bodies in the village. A grandmother who was the lynchpin of her family, who saw two of her sons and a daughter off to Canada before the war, then had to go to London when those two sons came back to the UK badly injured in the war, and who never saw her daughter again. Her grandmother also cared for another daughter (my mother's mother) who was ill and emotionally fragile all her life, and whose husband had left her, so that as a child my mother was not certain whether she really had a father or not. A grandmother who put the fear of God into my mother by descriptions of what might happen to her if she ventured far away from the village.

My mother used the expression, "It's living through it that's the difficult part". That has been the story of her life, but she has lived through it and now enjoys her family so much. She has been so excited every time one of her grandchildren has got married and adores having three great grandsons to visit her.

She recently remembered how Abi used to behave when we were visiting them. Abi would poke her head round their bedroom door and take one look at Grandpa in bed and make a dash right round the bed to the safety of Granny. Grandpa used to look different in bed because he was often without his glasses and his hair would be askew after a night's sleep: she just wasn't quite sure how to take him. My mother still recollects that behaviour, and clearly rejoiced in the fact that she was the 'safe' grandparent.

When I thought further about Abi's funeral, I wonder how selfish I was then. I didn't give anyone else a chance to do anything or say anything. I just wanted to give the little bunch of flowers to Abi and send her off on her way. I was a robot; I don't think I let any of my emotion out, because of the children. I desperately wanted to protect them, they were hurting, they didn't understand the consequences of what had happened. Neither did I. What I didn't want was for my children to have to protect me, to feel they couldn't cry or be upset in case it upset me further. Despite my best intentions, that is what happened. Maybe that is how it is. Families who love each other want to protect one another. The more love there is the more you want to protect.

The deeper the love you have, the deeper the capacity for pain. I have realised that many times over the years. I think it is something we have all experienced in our family.

Twelve

What I have Learned

It is now 2010 and over 25 years since Abi died. Between starting to write this book and where we are now is five years. Much has changed, whilst much has stayed the same.

My fears about what I was asking the family to do were, in the end, not realised. I think they all found it a therapeutic process, and certainly since then it has been much easier to talk about Abi naturally and I've noticed there is less visible upset around.

We have had many celebrations in the last few years: the weddings of each of our children, the birth of three grandchildren and the Diamond Wedding anniversary of my parents are just some of the significant milestones. Each of these events has been a tremendously happy occasion, but every time there has been a tinge of sadness. When I spoke at Matthew's wedding I emphasised the importance of the family and how we can all support one another. I mentioned those who were absent, and uppermost in my mind was Abi. In the run up to the preparations for each wedding (especially Cathy's in 2009) I often wondered what Abi's role would have been, what sort of young woman she would have turned out to be, how she would have loved to be a part of our happiness. What sort of aunt would she have been to Henry, James and Louis? When the whole family is together, I notice how Simon and Cathy play and interact with the three little boys. I feel incredibly proud of all of them – for the ways they have managed to release themselves from their past, the way in which they can lose themselves in playing football or rugby and manage small accidents between the boys.

Matthew's feelings about Abi being **'sacred'** echoed some of Paddy's thoughts about her. Paddy talked about the physical pain he has in his heart when he talks or thinks about her; he had that pain when she was alive but loved the feel of it. Now it's very hard for him. Part of the pain, I think, is that we feel it less and less with time. Abi has moved away from us, or we have moved away from her, and there is a gap. I think this process and the 'sacred' nature of Abi also echoes the private space we have each occupied since she died. She was an ordinary little girl and actually it's important to remember that and not inflate her with a sense of something she didn't have when she was alive. I think there is an idea, that we all have in our different ways, of Abi being 'sacred' in some way and of being very special to us individually. Of course we each had our own relationships with her that were unique to the two of us, but in a sense the holding on to the specific relationships we each had resulted in us feeling isolated and maybe contributed to the gap.

As I have sorted things out and tidied up, I have come across memories of her. Very recently, I found a collection of her clothing which I had kept. Her dressing gown and slippers from when she went into hospital, a dress I remember her wearing, a blanket she used to have in her cot. I knew where I had kept them, but something yesterday made Paddy suggest that we put them carefully into a shoe-box at the bottom of our blanket chest. He said he thought that would be a nice surprise for our children when they are sorting out our possessions after we have both died. I'm not sure – I wonder if they will think we are morbid, if we should have recycled them in some way. Now it won't be a surprise anyway...

And I still sometimes find at the bottom of a drawer a pad with scribbles on it which were her early attempts at drawing. There are several places where I know I will come across reminders of Abi: a little hat she used to wear; a cardboard roll which she had drawn on to make into a bracelet not long before she died; her identity bracelet from when she was born; locks of her blonde, silky hair which were cut off when she was in hospital. Just as there are bits and pieces which belong to the other children around the house, so there are with her too.

Recently, a friend I hadn't seen for a long time saw a photo of our niece and wondered if it was Abi. She told me how she still has a photo of Abi, playing with her son when they were quite small – I was so pleased that she lives on in other people's memories as well as mine.

Yet again I am writing this in the run up to the anniversary of her death. There is always a poignancy to this time of year, the days drawing in, leaves falling, the smell of bonfires in the air. A little death in itself as the summer fades away and winter approaches. Yet somehow each year still feels a small victory; another year accomplished with happy memories in spite of the loss which never leaves us. And increasingly the years seem to become more filled with happiness for us all as the family grows.

If Abi had lived would we have really treasured our happiness and what we have achieved as a family? Maybe not, maybe we would have been complacent and not understood how quickly and devastatingly our sense of ourselves as a unit could be destroyed. I believe that we know how lucky we are, how we appreciate what we have – the relationships, the love we have for one another. Sometimes it lessens, and I know that sometimes I don't sufficiently appreciate my life and all it contains. I do consider myself a lucky woman, with all I have, all I have worked for and created. But it can sometimes feel like a stretch to describe myself as lucky, given the huge loss and gap still in my life.

I believe that one of the things Abi has given me is the chance to think deeply about who I am, what I do, how I work and what I offer to those I work with. I trust I can help others to some small degree, that I can empathise with them, that I can offer them some sort of understanding. Most importantly, I hope I can give that understanding to my children and grandchildren. Henry, James and Louis have all been instrumental in helping us as a family to move on.

This process will never end – all our lives are inextricably linked together of course and I wouldn't want it any other way. Yet I have noticed how over the last couple of years Abi has faded from me to some degree. The memories are less vivid; it is more rare for the pain of her loss to arise and it is not so acute. I am unsure what to put this down to. Partly my life has taken on a new phase – Paddy is retired, I am working less, we have three grandchildren, my parents now live 50 yards from our house. My life is busier in many ways than when I worked full-time. Life is, in fact, very rewarding.

I continue to have insights, reflections and understandings about what I have learnt and how I have assimilated the loss of Abi into my life. But I need to put a stop to this writing at some point. I want the finished product to be available and not always to be in process, though I do want to keep on learning and understanding. In order for me to begin writing this book, I had to do some more deep personal work. I had help from friends and colleagues that then gave me the strength to ask the family for their memories and recollections. I had to find a way to access the internal resilience to ask the questions, listen to the answers without feeling guilty or defensive, and have an understanding of what Abi's death meant to them.

I have learned a tremendous amount about bereavement since Abi died, both for myself and understanding much more about how it can affect the relationships of those who are 'left behind'. Everybody's experience of bereavement is different, and as I have said elsewhere, there are no right and wrong ways to live with it. Having said that, there are some things that have been born out of my own bereavement that have been consistently helpful for the people I have worked with in the course of my job as a counsellor. I include them here both as a reminder for myself and as guiding principles that others might find helpful.

Remember that you will be far more tired than usual. Grieving is the most energy-depleting experience I have known. It is difficult when people come to visit because they will take their lead from you and that is an exhausting process. Feel strong enough to say you need to rest and lie down alone, or with someone to hold you.

Don't drive unless you really have to. Recognise that your reflexes will be much slower than normal; Paddy and I both bumped our car at different points after Abi died just because our mind wasn't on driving. We were thinking (or not thinking) about something much more important.

Make sure you have something to eat. Even if you don't feel like it, your body needs nourishment. People are likely to ask what they can do for you – ask them to bring some food which you can heat up easily and don't have to worry about.

Talk as much as you can to as many people as you can. I was so lucky with one particular very close friend who managed to make time to see me every day even though she herself had a big family to look after. She listened to me talking it over and over as long as I liked, or not talking about it. Perhaps those friends are one in a million, I don't know.

Find at least one person you can be quiet with, who won't feel uncomfortable with silence. I had Paddy but the friend above was this person for me too, as well as being so generous with her time.

Remember it's OK to ask people to come back another time, or to ring later. You could always put a note on your front door saying that, rather than crawling round on the floor like I did to avoid people seeing me!

Don't feel bad about avoiding others. You can't function with other people all the time.

And it's OK not to feel 'brave' – whatever that means.

Whatever you decide to do is the right thing for you. If you want to empty your home of the person's possessions that's OK and, equally, if you want to hang onto them, that's OK too.

Time is meaningless. Particular anniversaries may have a special significance and the first year will be full of them – all those anniversaries are likely to feel like an ordeal to be got through. You don't 'get over' a death in a finite time; it takes as long as it takes.

Don't listen to people who try to tell you that you will feel better in a year, or two years. If you remember that, and then you don't feel stronger, you may feel guilty. Don't feel guilty.

Your belief about what happens when a loved one dies is the right one for you. Don't feel bad if others try to put their faith onto you and you reject it. Let them use their faith for themselves; for them to grieve in their own way.

Believe in yourself – you know what to do for yourself and those closest to you.

I feel a very lucky woman. I have been loved and supported all my life by family and friends. I had the wonderful gift of five children and even though two of those children didn't live to share much of their lives with the rest of us, what they did give me has enabled me to become fulfilled in my life. Their presence in my life has meant I am able to do the work I do, with whatever skills I have. I wouldn't have been without those experiences ever.

So thank you Abi, and baby daughter before you, for everything...

Thirteen

A Letter to my Daughter

Abi and dandelion

Dear Abi,

I wonder if you would like to know what happened to us all after you died. How we coped without you. How we are living our lives now. Would you like to know how we remember you, and how important you have always been to all of us in our own ways?

You were, and are, so special to all of us. Even now, all these years later, people remember you and they mention

225

you from time to time if they think we won't get too upset. Your life and death played such an important part in our lives. I think there were times when we all felt we didn't know how we would carry on without you. You brought us so much joy and laughter and when you died the light went out. The house, which had seemed so noisy and full of children, felt empty, hollow. It was like a shell, it's hard to believe that a little child like you had so much effect.

Playing on the radio just now is *'I never met a girl like you before'* and that's true – never before, nor since. I felt so proud of you all the time you were in my life, and proud of me too, I suppose, having brought you safely into the world. I loved being pregnant with you, even though I spent quite a lot of the time frightened that something terrible would happen to the baby inside me. That was because I didn't know you then, you were just a growing baby, and I didn't realise the strength and determination you had which meant you would come into our lives and almost take charge! You were so bright and bubbly; you filled another dimension in our family.

The gap was huge when you left. And I had so many questions that never got answered. Not that I expect you will answer them now. Why did you come to us? What was the point of it all? What did you bring us? What would I learn? How would I cope? How could I bring up the others to be happy children and adults? You would never have had the answers of course, being the youngest, but somehow I felt you held the answers, and without you I couldn't do it. By that I mean carry on being a Mum to your brothers and sister, a happy wife for your Dad, be happy myself and find fulfilment in my life. But I have. I feel proud of that: when I look at the other three now they are all strong confident adults forging their relationships and careers in different ways.

But it's been a hard journey for them and they have missed you just as much as Dad and I have. A lot of the time has been very isolating. We have all felt alone, and we have had to learn how to cope on our own. We have all realised that it's a solitary process; no-one else can really help that much.

I think we all put so much importance onto you and that was unfair. We put a mythic quality to you, when in fact you were a normal little girl achieving the usual milestones. It is as if you did no wrong when you were alive, and of course that isn't true, as you'll remember!

Today there are three little boys, Henry, James and Louis, who will never know you. One day Matthew will tell them that they would have had another aunt. I guess they will think that you would be like Cathy is, but we know that isn't the case. You would have been different; you would have had another kind of relationship with them. You would have loved them! They are so beautiful, so full of life and such a wonderful gift. Matthew is a great father and he loves Olivia so much. You would have loved her too, I am sure, and she would have loved having another sister-in-law.

Do you remember how you used to love playing energetic games with Matthew and Simon? Henry and James are just the same as you, and Louis, when he is a bit older, will join in with the rough and tumble. Henry has such a gorgeous laugh and a way of looking at people that reminds me of you.

I am so thrilled that I can just love those three little boys now with all my heart. I have learnt how to do that now, when I had years of thinking I would never be able to. It was so hard for me seeing other little children being so lively and happy, when all I wanted was to have you with me, in my arms again to give me such a big hug. I have understood that I am not disloyal to you by being happy now. That is what you would have wanted.

Abi, thank you for being my daughter. It was wonderful, exciting, heart-breaking, all at the same time. I wouldn't have missed it for the world.

With all my love, your Mum xxx

Appendix

Alison's Commonplace Book

It is not growing like a tree
in bulk, doth make men better be;
Or standing long an oak,
three hundred years.
To fall a log at last,
dry, bald and sere.
A lily of a day,
Is fairer far in May.
Although it fall and die that night,
It was the plant and flower of light.
In small proportions,
we just beauties see;
And in small measures,
life may perfect be.

Ben Jonson

From
Lydia Ramage

What is pink? A rose is pink
by the fountain's brink
What is red? A poppy's red
On its barley bed
What is blue? The sky is blue
Where the clouds float through
What is white? A swan is white
sailing in the light.
What is yellow? A pear is yellow
rich and ripe and mellow.
What is green? The grass is green
with small flowers between.
What is violet? The clouds are violet
in the summer twilight.
What is orange? Why, an orange
Just an orange.

Christina Rossetti

Read by Cathy
at Abi's
celebration
meeting
November 1984

And a woman who held a babe against her bosom said,
Speak to us of Children.
And he said:
Your children are not your children.
They are the sons and daughters of Life's longing for itself.
They come through you but not from you,
And though they are with you yet they belong
not to you.

You may give them your love but not your thoughts,
For they have their own thoughts.
You may house their bodies but not their souls,
For their souls dwell in the house of to-morrow,
which you cannot visit, not even in your dreams.
You may strive to be like them,
but seek not to make them like you.
For life goes not backward nor tarries with yesterday.
You are the bows from which your children as
living arrows are sent forth.

The archer sees the mark upon the path of the
infinite, and He bends you with His might that
His arrows may go swift and far.
Let your bending in the Archer's hand be for gladness;
For even as He loves the arrow that flies,
so He loves also the bow that is stable.

From The Prophet – Khalil Gibran

Is it not strange that an infant should be heir of the world, and see those mysteries which the books of the learned never unfold.
Thomas Traherne

He said not: thou shalt not be travailed, thou shalt not be afflicted: but he said: thou shalt not be overcome. **Mother Julian**

In every thing there is a season, and a time to every purpose under the heaven.
Ecclesiastes 3:1

As much as in a hundred years she's dead
Yet is today the day on which she died. **D.G.Rossetti**

And ever has it been that love knows not its own depth until the hour of separation.
The Prophet

If I should die and leave you here awhile,
Be not like others sore, undone,
Who keep long vigil by the silent dust and weep
For my sake, turn again to life and smile,
Nerving thy heart and trembling hand
To do something to comfort other hearts than thine
Complete these dear unfinished tasks of mine,
And I, perchance, may therein comfort you.

Unknown

Do not stand at my grave and weep –
I am not there – I do not sleep
I am a thousand winds that blow,
I am the softly falling snow,
I am the gentle rains that fall,
I am the fields of ripening grain.
I am in the morning hush
I am in the graceful rush
Of beautiful birds in circling flight.
I am the starshine of the night.
I am in the flowers that bloom
I am in a quiet room.
I am in the birds that sing
I am in each lovely thing.
Do not stand at my grave
and cry – I did not die...

Mary E. Frye 1932

Never say in grief
He is no more
Only say in thankfulness
He was

Unknown

Bring us, O Lord, at our last awakening, into the house and gate of heaven, to enter into that gate and dwell in that house where there shall be no darkness nor dazzling, but one equal light: no noise nor silence, but one equal music: no fears nor hopes, but one equal possession: no ends or beginnings, but one equal eternity in the habitation of thy glory and dominion, world without end.

John Donne

Another misery there is in affection; that whom we truly love like our own selves, we forget their looks, nor can our memory retain the idea of their faces, and it is no wonder, for they are ourselves, and our affection makes their looks our own.

Sir Thomas Browne

I wither daily – time touches her not.

Unknown

I looked for her in the garden for she was always there, somewhere out of reach, out of sight, always with me. She was who she was, entirely herself, for that brief time, who knows what she would have become.

Unknown

You will never forget her or stop loving her. You will think of her every single day of your life.

Unknown

Heaviness may endure for a night, but joy cometh in the morning.

Psalm 30:5

Do the duty that is nearest to thee.

Unknown

When you are sorrowful look again in your heart, and you shall see that in truth you are weeping for that which has been your delight.

The Prophet

When sorrows come, they come not single spies
But in battalions.

William Shakespeare, Hamlet

You give but little when you give of your possessions.
It is when you give of yourself that you truly give.

Unknown

Remember me when I am gone away
Gone far away into the silent land
When you can no more hold me by the hand
Nor I half turn to go – yet turning stay;
Remember when no more day by day
You tell me of our future that you planned
Only remember me; you understand
It will be late to counsel then or pray.
Yet if you should forget me for a while,
And, afterwards remember, do not grieve.
For if the darkness and corruption leave,
A vestige of the thoughts that once I had
Better by far, you should forget and smile
Than that you should remember and be sad.

Christina Rossetti

In perfect honour, perfect truth,
And gentleness to all mankind.
You trod the golden paths of youth
Then left the world and youth behind.
Ah no! 'tis we who fade and fail –
And you, from times slow torments free,
Shall pass from strength to strength and scale
The steeps of immortality.

John Buchan *Frati Dilectissimo*

Significant Dates

1966 Christine and Paddy meet through Quakers in Newcastle.

1967–1971 Christine trains as a nurse in London while Paddy is a medical student in Birmingham.

1971 Christine and Paddy marry in December.

1973 Matthew is born in Birmingham. Paddy is a junior hospital doctor. Christine stops working to become a full-time Mum.

1975 Cathy is born in Wolverhampton. The family moves to Hull when she is six weeks old.

1976 Paddy's father Gerald dies.

1977 Family move to Bishop Auckland, Co. Durham while Paddy works in general practice for a year.

1978 Simon is born. The family moves to Dundee when he is three weeks old. Paddy returns to hospital medicine.

1980 Our fourth baby is due in early August. 13th July Christine falls and badly breaks her arm, the baby girl is stillborn on 15th July.

1981 Abigail Clare is born on 10th December by Caesarean section.

1983 The family returns to Hull in March when Paddy begins working in the Department of Medicine for the Elderly at Hull Royal Infirmary.

1984 Abi dies on 16th November.

1987-9 Christine and Paddy undergo intervention treatment in the hope of another pregnancy.

1990 Christine undertakes a 'Back to Nursing' course and after applying for several jobs, is appointed as a Practice Nurse at the University Health Centre (a general practice which cared for students predominantly) in Hull. This post expands its hours and commitment.

1992 Christine begins counselling training and development with the Oasis School of Human Relations. This leads to her building a counselling practice within the general practice and finding that this is what she wants to do for her work in the future.

1994 Christine has an early miscarriage.

1994 to date Christine continues to develop her work as a mentor, counsellor and from 1999 becomes a co-Director of The Oasis School of Human Relations.

1997 Paddy's mother Marley dies.

2006 Matthew and Olivia marry; Henry is born.

2007 Christine becomes a non-Executive Director of Oasis and takes up part-time work.

2008 James is born.

2009 Simon and Claire marry and Cathy and Simon marry. Paddy retires.

2010 Louis is born. Anthony and Alison move house to York to be near the family.

Acknowledgements

I have had immense encouragement and support from all my family during the writing of this book. They have given me their contributions generously and never pushed me to produce the final product.

Very special thanks go to Heather Tweddle and Helen Coyle who between them offered extremely helpful suggestions to drafts of this book. Their careful editing has improved it immeasurably. Also my thanks to the readers who gave me useful comments and such encouraging feedback.

I am lucky to have many supportive and loving friends who have given me much over the years. To everyone at Oasis, friends from Hull and other parts of the country – thank you for all you have given me.

Paddy and I spent many hours discussing the impact of Abi's death. We intimately dissected our individual experiences. We had times of intense grief, times of sorrow at our loss and times of laughter and real joy when we remembered our family life as it was when Abi was alive. The changes in our family structure have meant that, over time, we have been able to participate and enjoy family life once again.

Paddy has loved and supported me since I was 16 and so my deepest thanks go to him for always believing in me.

Chris Neligan
August 2011

Charitable Donations from the sale of
Life is But a Dream

Burkitt's Lymphoma is a common cancer in central Africa, usually affecting children, and is strongly linked to reduced resistance to a virus called the Epstein-Barr virus (which causes glandular fever in teenagers in the UK). The jawbone is often involved causing skull and facial deformities.

Children may present for medical treatment late in the disease process and already have deformities that are not curable. However the cancer can be cured by using chemotherapy drugs which destroy the cancer cells. The cost of treatment for each child is relatively small.

Shortly before she died Abigail was deeply affected by television pictures of starving children in Africa, the scenes that prompted Bob Geldof to set up Live-Aid. When she died we organised a collection in her memory to send to help those children.

A donation from the sale of each copy of this book is paid through ODEF (Oasis Development Education Foundation) to a fund at Hospice Africa Uganda earmarked specifically for treatment of Burkitt's Lymphoma.

Chris Neligan is Chair of ODEF, and another Oasis Director, Zena Bernacca, is on secondment as CEO of Hospice Africa Uganda for 12 months in 2011 - 2012.